CONQUER
— THE —
POST-COLLEGE
PASSION-SLUMP

Success Secrets to Thrive in Your 20's, 30's, and Beyond

JASON HEINRITZ

www.DailyLifeUniversity.com

Conquer the Post-College Passion Slump
Success Secrets to THRIVE in your 20s, 30s & Beyond
Jason Heinritz

SELF-PUBLISHING
SCHOOL

NOW IT'S YOUR TURN

Discover the EXACT 3-step blueprint you need to become a bestselling author in 3 months.

Self-Publishing School helped me, and now I want them to help you with this FREE VIDEO SERIES!

Even if you're busy, bad at writing, or don't know where to start, you CAN write a bestseller and build your best life.

With tools and experience across a variety niches and professions, Self-Publishing School is the only resource you need to take your book to the finish line!

DON'T WAIT

Watch this FREE VIDEO SERIES now, and
Say "YES" to becoming a bestseller:

https://xe172.isrefer.com/go/curcust/heinritzjr28

DEDICATION

I dedicate my first book to the love of my life, Abby. She is my biggest supporter. She challenges me to be a better man every day.

I am blessed and thankful to be surrounded by a great support system of wonderful church friends, work friends, and family.

I am extremely grateful for my launch team! They helped get the word out about this book and help my dream of being an author a reality.

I am very lucky to have found a great editor to make me sound much better than I am. Thank you Emily Schutte!

This book is also dedicated to Cutco Cutlery. I would not have the mindset to write this book without the lessons learned at Cutco. I would not have met the leaders who became invaluable guides. And I would not have known the value of investing in myself, the practices upon which this book was conceived.

This book is also dedicated to Hal Elrod and Chandler Boldt. Hal paved the way for me with his book, *The Miracle Morning,* and gave me confidence that if he can do it, so can I. Chandler Boldt and Self-Publishing School gave me the program and tools necessary to turn this book into reality.

A Special Invitation from Jason

Fans and readers of this book – just like you – make up an extraordinary community of like-minded individuals who wake up each day fueled by a dedication to fulfilling their unlimited potential.

As creator of the *Daily Life University* program, it is my responsibility to create an online space where individuals can connect, find encouragement, share best practices, offer and receive support, post videos, develop discipline and accountability, and even discuss this book.

The mission of *Daily Life University* is to create a community of over 100,000 members from around the world. To help us meet that goal, visit and join our official Facebook group, *Daily Life University Community – Students of Life.* There, you'll be able to connect with like-minded individuals who are already students of life. You'll find daily motivation from our inspirational posts and videos to help accelerate your success.

I am personally moderating and encouraging this community.

I look forward to seeing you there.

- Jason

CONTENTS

Breakfast

Read This Book If You Don't Want to Live an Average Life

Hello. Thank yourself for taking the time to read this book.

If you are a high school or college student who wants to get the most out of your future, you should read this book.

If you're enrolled in college but you're not motivated enough to attend classes or do your homework, you should read this book.

If you are disappointed about spending four years at a university only to walk away with a piece of paper that gives you no guarantee for success, you should read this book.

If you are a college graduate but don't feel like you have the life skills you need to succeed in the real world, you should read this book.

If you graduated and have tens of thousands of dollars of debt and haven't found a job in your related field, you should read this book.

If you're a young professional looking to continually grow and improve yourself, you should read this book.

If you are somebody who wants to leave your 20s ahead of the majority, then *get excited* about reading this book.

In her book, *The Defining Decade: Why Your Twenties Matter — And How to Make the Most of Them Now,* University of Virginia clinical psychologist Meg Jay argues that the first years of adulthood are the most important time in a young person's life. The 20s are a crucial age for both college graduates and non-college graduates:

> *We know that 80 percent of life's most defining moments happen by age 35. We know that 70 percent of lifetime wage growth happens in the first 10 years of a career. We know that more than half of Americans are married or living with or dating their future partner by 30. Our personalities change more in our 20s than any other time. Our fertility peaks. Our brain caps off its last growth spurts. The things that we do and the things that we don't do are going to have an enormous effect across years and even generations.*
>
> *Twenty-somethings are worried. They're anxious. They're worried about whether life is going to work out for them. Whether it's going to work out as well as they thought it would. But the thing to do about that is to realize that my 20s are really the time to make my own certainty, and to make sure that yes, my life is going to work out because I'm starting to put the pieces together in an intentional way.*
>
> *There are 50 million twenty-somethings in the United States most of whom are living with a staggering, unprecedented amount of uncertainty. Many no idea what they will be doing, where they will be living, or who they will be within 2 or 10 years. They don't know when they'll be happy or when they will be able to pay their bills. They wonder if they should be photographers or lawyers or event planners. They don't know whether they are a few dates or many years from a*

meaningful relationship. They worry about whether they will have families or whether their marriages will last. Most simply, they don't know whether their lives will work out and they don't know what to do. Uncertainty makes people anxious and distraction is the 21st-Century opiate of the masses. So too many 20 somethings are tempted, and even encouraged, to just turn away and hope for the best. That's not the way to go. [1]

I am writing this book to help develop young leaders in America. I have noticed a disconnect between what colleges teach and what is really needed after graduation. After spending five years at the University of Wisconsin – Whitewater, where I received a great education, I nonetheless found myself with a five-year degree, a piece of paper, and thousands of dollars in debt.

I watched most of my friends waste their time in college, failing to use the opportunities it offered to grow as a person and develop in all of the areas Meg describes. They graduated with a piece of paper, thinking that they would be set for life.

The harsh reality is that a lot of our future success is not based on what we learn in the classroom.

I see most young people developing bad habits, staying out too late, and failing to take these crucial years more seriously. The "YOLO" culture is a perfect example.

To clarify, I am not advocating against higher education. I fully recognize that college is very important to many career paths. What I find much more important, however, are the people skills and life skills one develops while navigating post-high school life. This includes the mistakes they make (and learn from), and the habits they create to be successful. The skills young

3

people learn as they mature into adults and the relationships they build last a lifetime. In this stage of life, some may even find their future spouse or make a connection that leads to their dream job.

One of the biggest problems I see with today's college culture is *who* and *what* surrounds young people in their post-high school years. Therefore, this book is written to impact individuals in their 20's and 30's. It is meant to be a supplement to your college education and young professional life.

Here's the reality: if college students spent just one hour a day growing as a person instead of partying, sleeping, watching TV, or playing video games, our society would be filled with more leaders and fewer followers. Society would be filled with better husbands and wives, friends, co-workers, and leaders who are prepared to make a difference.

Through this book, I'll be teaching a series of "courses." Each is designed to help you learn and grow. You will spend less time studying than you would in a college course but the results will be far more impactful than the *Geography of Coffee* class you took your sophomore year.

I am very fortunate and blessed to have been raised by a supportive mother and father in a wonderful Christian home. I learned a lot of early lessons from my parents and growing up in the church. I was also very fortunate that at the age of 19, I started working for a direct sales company called Cutco Cutlery. After my freshman year of college, thanks to my success with the company, I realized the value of personal growth.

I learned how to work with people, how to negotiate, how to set schedules and stick to them. I learned how to build value in products and services, and help others recognize it. I learned how to run a business. I learned how to be a leader, how to overcome adversity, and how not to trade time for money. Most importantly,

I learned that my new degree in personal development would lead to a greater degree of success than any college degree ever could.

Before working at Cutco, I never cared about reading books or personal growth. I cared more about playing video games and watching sports. But by age 20, I understood the importance of reading books and going to seminars.

Since starting Cutco, I have read 100+ books on personal growth topics and becoming a better person. I have attended more than 60+ conferences on personal development. Over the last 10+ years, I realized that the information I learned from books and conferences was not taught in college. This book goes hand-in-hand with a college education.

Whether you are attending college, stuck in a job you don't like, living in the basement of your parents' house, or working at a fast food joint, this book will be the *Daily Life University* that you need to set yourself up for a better future.

Before you start reading...

Take this quick self-assessment, called the Circle of Life. This will help you be more aware of what you want to improve as you navigate this book!

Directions: The eight sections in the Wheel of Life represent different aspects of your life. Seeing the center of the wheel as 1 and the outer edges as 10, rank your level of satisfaction with each life area by drawing a straight or curved line to create a new outer edge. The new perimeter represents the wheel of your life. If this were a real wheel, how bumpy would the ride be? [2]

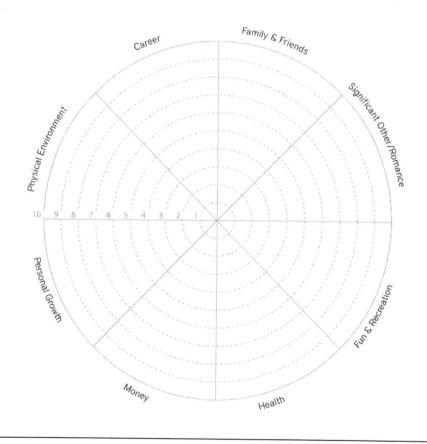

How to Read this Book

This book is written like a study guide for an important test – and the most important test is the test of life. Think of this book like a college course. Take notes, highlight and write all over it, and use it to capture and expand your ideas, realizations, and thoughts.

This book can be very powerful when read with a friend. Mark this book, compare notes with each other, and hold each other accountable. And when you're done reading this book, go back and look at your notes and highlights, and remember the key takeaways. Just like being in a class with friends, make it a point to get together for study sessions to truly apply the material.

At the end of each course, you have assignments. Don't think of these assignments as annoying or boring, but as challenges to stretch your mind, build discipline, and rise above the average.

By holding this book, you are signing up for the course of life. You are preparing for the many challenges life will inevitably bring.

Congratulations. And welcome to the *Daily Life University*.

PART 1

WHY BECOME A STUDENT OF LIFE

COURSE 1

What Your Parents Taught You
(Because They Were Part of the Same System)

In this course, you'll uncover the truth about what your parents taught you. Not to learn that they taught you anything wrong, but to realize that their example has an effect on everything you believe to be true. You will explore the ripple effect of your mind being filled with your parents' ideas.

We are all products of our past, which includes our upbringing.

But that does not mean we have to be prisoners of our past.

We may be where we are today because of our upbringing; however, this doesn't prevent a successful future.

Think about it: you are who you are because of the guidance of a select few people who raised you, mainly through trial and error. Those people are your parents. They may have the best intentions for you. But, just like you, they are human and don't always do what's best.

The reason this lesson is so important is because your parents were raised in a different era. Compared to 40 years ago, today might as well be a different planet. Things you love and can't live without – computers, mobile phones, this thing called the Internet, etc. – didn't exist during your parents' upbringing.

Your parents were not raised to trust online shopping. Many are still figuring out how and why to use texting – although once they do, it seems they don't stop – and prefer face-to-face conversations.

The point is that your parents were brought up in a different time. They are probably part of the Baby Boomer generation (born between 1946 and 1964) or Generation X (born between 1962 and 1982).

Baby Boomers and Gen Xers are hard workers. Their upbringing includes the boom of the 9-to-5 lifestyle. As a result, many spent decades working on a factory floor or became blue-collar workers. They learned to avoid the risks that come with leaving their 9-to-5 pensions, raises, and security. And today, they still don't. Your parents probably prefer stability and are skeptical of ideas outside the 9-to-5 system.

Baby Boomers and Gen Xers have been, in one way, raised by the government, guided by school systems to follow orders and rules, and trained to stick to that path. They believe in the "safe route": going to school, getting into college, graduating, getting a good job, getting married, buying a house, having kids, and living happily ever after. But today's fast-paced, flexible, and rarely stable reality is far different from the world our parents were born into.

Yet each of us makes decisions and creates beliefs based on our parents' example. We watch them make a decision or express an opinion and accept it as truth. But we don't consider that, just maybe, their decisions and beliefs aren't really theirs. Just like you, *their* parents, teachers, bosses, and significant others served as examples to follow. And, just like you, they may not even realize it.

Here's a story to illustrate my point:

Joan is a young newlywed who wants to make her husband his first homemade dinner. She tries her hand at her grandmother's brisket recipe. Her grandmother always cut off the ends of the roast. And so, Joan cuts off the ends just like her grandmother always does. The meat is delicious, but after dinner her husband asks, "Why do you cut off the ends, that's the best part!" She answers, "That's the way my grandmother always made it."

The next week, they visit Joan's grandmother and she prepares her famous brisket recipe, cutting off the ends like she always does. Joan, curious that she must be missing some vital piece of information, asks her grandmother why she cuts off the ends. Her grandma says, "That's the only way it will fit in the pan!"[3]

As you read, Joan was just following her grandmother's recipe. Little did she know, her grandma had limited options and was making the most of what she had. Grandma's options at the time didn't make sense for Joan's current situation. Joan was blindly following her grandma's example without understand the "why" behind it.

Now that you've read this course, you realize that your parents can only teach you what *they* were taught, which may not always be the best if you want to move with today's ever-changing times.

In the next lesson, you'll find out how you're negatively influenced by constant, daily screen time.

Course 1 Assignments

1. Write about one thing you realize your parents didn't really understand or believe in, but passed down to you because "that's just how it is."

2. Think about an old way of thinking that has been passed down from your family or school system. Is it relevant today? If you could, would you choose a new way of thinking?

The Screen Daze:
We Are Becoming Media Zombies

In the second lesson, you'll open your eyes to the harsh reality of how most young people are learning today and realize how society influences us.

Leaders are very intentional about who and what they allow to influence them. But many people are educated by what they see on their screens. As a nation, we are glued to our TVs, phones, and computers.

Most news you read, watch, or listen to is not positive or encouraging. Turn on talk radio or the morning news for five minutes and you can easily become depressed. Typically, the news is made up of catastrophes, missing persons, bankruptcies, school shootings, and the many other things wrong with our nation. Yes, there is a quick minute of sports and weather. But by 8:00 a.m., you already need a "pick me up" to survive the rest of the day.

**We spend hours each day looking at other people's lives
rather than improving our own.**

What if you stopped sitting in front of the TV? What would your life look like? How much time would you save? What could you do instead?

Yet today, most of us have a virtual life: We stay up late, we get a late start, and we don't give ourselves time to reflect and think.

Our Addiction to Social Media

"I'm an addict.

This addiction consumes my life. It affects my health. It stresses my relationships. It affects my work performance. I prefer to lay in bed and fuel my addiction rather than get up and live my life. I would rather stay inside, by myself with my addiction, than get out and socialize with other people. I constantly sneak in quick fixes around friends, during work meetings, even in line at the grocery store.

My addiction isn't drugs or alcohol, or any of the common compulsive behaviors. And even though my behavior isn't illegal, it may be just as threatening to my life.

My name is Jason and I'm addicted to social media."

Do you find yourself relating to any of these struggles?

Most of our days start with the sound of a phone alarm, and end with a final check of social media on that same phone. The digital world has never been more accessible, in any time or place, thanks to our phones. And we bring these accessories with us everywhere – yes, even the restroom. Those few minutes you spent passing the latest level of a digital game can sometimes seem to play a crucial role in improving your day. Even eating dinner can be hard to enjoy when scrolling through Facebook is an arm's length away.

We are addicted to our mobile devices. Millennials check their phones over 85 times a day. One of the most powerful resources I have seen on this epidemic is a video called *Look Up*. It portrays a very realistic take on social media and its effect on society: "*This media we call social is anything but when we open our computers and it's our doors we shut.*"[4]

Imagine all the things you miss while you're staring at your phone. Here's a piece of advice from *Look Up*: "*So look up from your phone, shut down the display, take in your surroundings, make the most of today, just one real connection is all it can take to show you the difference being there can make.*"[4]

So how do you reduce your social media addiction? Here are some activities – or "games" – to help you, starting tonight. The next time you're in a social setting, suggest one of the following games:

Phone Pile – Tell your friends to put their phone into a pile in the middle of the table. The first person to reach for and grab their phone loses. Get creative with the consequences. You could make them play truth or dare, pay for dinner or drinks, or turn off their phone.

Social Media Phone Dare – Unlike like the first game, this one lets everyone keep his or her phones. But if someone gets caught checking social media, the person who catches him or her gets to choose the consequence. Once again, get creative with the "punishment."

"Ear Candy"

You are not only influenced by what you see, but also by what you hear. Have you ever heard the phrase, "In one ear, out the other"? It's not entirely accurate. I like to say, "In one ear, ingrained into your brain, and definitely not out the other."

As sweet as candy tastes, it's bad for your health. After the initial pleasure of that sweet, sugary taste, it produces zero value towards your long-term well-being.

That's what most of us are doing with our ears. We fill our minds with "ear candy." Whether it's TV or music, it's just something to entertain us for the moment which fails to bring any true value to our lives.

I still love watching a good episode of *Game of Thrones* or jamming out to *Justin Timberlake*. However, I realize that what I fill my mind with really matters. I was in the gym the other day watching ESPN and heard, for the sixth time, a story about off-field issues of NFL players. I realized how tired I was of hearing the same story in six different ways. I get it; it's attention-grabbing media, but I no longer choose to fill my mind with that negative information over and over.

As interesting as it is to watch and listen to five hours of pre-game shows, does any of that truly matter? Instead of watching five hours of pre-game coverage that week, *what if you worked on yourself?*

What would investing five hours a week of reading, studying, exercising, or improving a relationship do for your life?

Music today is mainly about sex, drugs, alcohol, problems, and hate. Although the songs may have a good beat, they do not add value to your future. There is a song from an artist named Lecrae, called *Sayin Nuthin*. The song talks about how most songs aren't positive, and based on the lyrics, they actually fill your mind with negative influences. [5]

This is why I try to listen to *K-Love* radio or podcasts in my car. It may not always be the coolest beat to jam to, but it does bring positivity to my life. And I recognize the value of the trade-off.

What if you just spent **20 minutes** a day listening to uplifting, life-improving material? Most of you can do this on your commute to school or work, or while you're at the gym. That adds up to **121 hours** a year.

What do you think would happen to you after hearing 121 hours of material about improving relationships, health, and becoming a better person? How different would your life be?

In this course, you learned the harsh reality of what screens and sounds are doing to you. You learned why so many people stay mediocre and don't break away from the masses.

In the next course, you'll understand why people think this way. You'll also learn why so many are misguided by the idea that all we need is a formal education – without self-education.

Course 2 Assignments

1. Watch the *Look Up* video: https://youtu.be/Z7dLU6fk9QY. [4]

2. Play one of the cell phone games the next time you hang out with friends.

3. Track your screen time with the *Moment App* on your cell phone:

    a. Your guess for the next seven days: _____ hours

    b. Actual time spent looking at a screen: _____ hours

Why Staying a Student After School Is So Important

In this lesson, you will learn the importance of ongoing education. Yes, you're probably thinking, "Wait...really? I was really hoping to *not* be a student ever again. I thought I was done learning and reading books after school." But this is not the case if you want to be an extraordinary individual.

Many of us think education stops after high school or college. That mentality is what keeps the average person mediocre. Yet just by reading this book, you're already choosing not to be average.

In November 2012, I attended a Tony Robbins event called *Unleash The Power Within* (UPW). Tony is considered one of the foremost experts on personal growth. It was a life-changing experience.

I was in a tough spot in my life and really needed a change. One of the concepts he shared is called "CANI," which stands for "Constant And Never-Ending Improvement." And it changed how I looked at self-improvement.

As human beings, we're constantly making mistakes, yet we should always be learning and growing. Most lessons are learned through trial and error, so don't be afraid to fail and welcome the improvement that follows.

If you don't use it, you lose it.

Just like working out, this applies to your brain. Too many young people damage their brains with video games, drugs, and alcohol. Your brain isn't growing and developing while you're sitting in front of a screen.

According to an Iowa State University study, students who stare at a screen for more than two hours per day are twice as likely to be diagnosed with attention problems – which is worrying when you consider the average number of hours a child spends watching television or playing video games is 4.26 hours a day. [6]

Think back to when you were 16 and just learning to drive. Remember how many rules you could recite about driving? Everything was fresh in your mind. You knew how to parallel park, how to give right-of-way at four-way stops, and how to react to extreme driving situations. But today, we sometimes forget these rules because they are no longer fresh in our minds. Today, we mainly drive on autopilot.

This is just like personal growth. Realize that your life is made up of your years. Your years are made up your months. And your months are made up of your days. **Therefore, each day matters.** To challenge and grow your mind, you need to pursue constant improvements.

I founded *Daily Life University* because investing in your personal growth is not a "sometimes" or a "someday" thing – it is a daily choice. And it's amazing what you can get done on a daily basis if you make it a priority, which is why you need discipline to increase your growth and success.

In this lesson, you realized how important it is to continually grow if you want to be different from the mediocre majority.

In the next course, you'll see the reality faced by most people with just a college degree. You'll also get great tips on how to fit personal growth around your school and job.

Course 3 Assignment

1. Watch this funny video of Father Guido talking about what most people remember five years out of college: https://youtu.be/kO8x8eoU3L4. [7]

COURSE 4

What is the Reality of a College Degree Without Personal Growth?

In this course, you will learn what most people believe happens once they graduate with a piece of paper. Most naively assume they're all set! But you will realize how important it is to continue to develop as a person while you're still young.

Unfortunately, a college education is not as affordable as it used to be. According to a study by the *Wall Street Journal*, most students graduate with at least **$35,000 in debt.** The article continues:

> *"The average class of 2015 graduate with student-loan debt will have to pay back a little more than $35,000, according to an analysis of government data... Even adjusted for inflation, that's still more than twice the amount borrowers had to pay back two decades earlier."*[8]

Many students graduate with this $35,000 in debt in four years with little to guarantee a successful future. And that $35,000 is just the debt left over after what's *already* been paid. According to *CollegeBoard.org*, in 2016 the average cost of a 4-year education at a public college was nearly $40,000 while the average for a private institution was just under $134,000. [9]

Studies also show that **73 percent of college graduates don't land a job in their field of study**, according to the *Washington Post*. The same publication estimated that just 27 percent of college graduates have a job that is closely related to their major. [10]

That's interesting because in 2010, just 62 percent of U.S. graduates had a job that required a college degree. [10] Therefore, nearly 40 percent of college graduates didn't technically need extra schooling.

So, what do you do when the degree you spent four to five years earning doesn't pay off? Do you settle and accept the debt and new job, or do you learn to develop your talents and abilities, regardless of your education?

Here's the reality:

Your GPA in formal education will not guarantee a successful future.

You may have heard that the average American switches careers seven times. According to Forbes magazine, *"ninety-one percent of Millennials (born between 1977-1997) expect to stay in a job for less than three years [therefore] Millennials will have 15 to 20 jobs over the course of their working lives."*[11]

You're starting to see the point: The problem is that most young people go to college for four to five years, spend a lot of money to earn a degree, and, unfortunately, will never land their dream job. They usually end up switching jobs, lacking discipline, and ending up in the mediocre majority.

That's the most likely path young people face today. But why is it that some *can* become successful doctors, lawyers, or entrepreneurs, while others can't seem to keep a job for more than three years?

The common denominator among all of those factors is YOU.

You follow yourself into your future. So, if you develop bad habits today, those bad habits follow you to your next job, your next relationship, even to your next New Year's resolutions.

Most young people treat college the wrong way and walk away with really bad habits. The reality of who a young person is learning to become in colleges is scary. Imagine spending over four years of your life ingraining poor habits. Then, you graduate and try to become a successful and responsible individual, which is the opposite of what you've done for the last several years of your life.

This is what I've noticed most students learn in college:

1. How to watch hours of re-runs and reality TV.

2. How to see the same ESPN episode four times in 24 hours.

3. How to play hours of video games.

4. How to find everything out about a person on social media instead of talking to them.

5. How to not respect and listen to superiors.

6. How to have multiple uncommitted relationships.

7. How to find the laziest way to get things done.

8. How to make excuses.

9. How to procrastinate.

10. How to develop poor sleeping habits

11. How to binge drink.

12. How to be unhealthy.

13. How to experiment with drugs.

14. How to cram and immediately forget what you studied.

15. How to be lazy.

16. How to accumulate thousands of dollars in debt.

17. How to be negative.

18. How to follow the crowd.

19. How to develop poor financial habits.

20. How to know more chants for sports teams than dreams for their own future.

This is not the college's fault; it is the fault of the social culture in college. When a bunch of teenagers come together, with no parents in sight, and plenty of free time, there's going to be trouble. **This means college students are in desperate need of learning *life skills*.**

When I was a student at UW–Whitewater, I thought I was a reasonably responsible student. I was raised in a Christian home with great parents. I didn't have a drink of alcohol until I was 19. I was an athlete and decided I didn't want to fill my body with substances that could hinder my athletic ability. Yet, I still found myself indulging in the chaos of college.

It was March 2004, and my friends decided to plan a spring break trip. I thought it'd be great idea to experience a spring break. I thought to myself, "how can I go to college *without* going on a spring break trip? Daytona Beach instead of the cold spring air of Wisconsin? Sign me up!"

In the weeks leading up to spring break, I realized there was going to be a lot of drinking. So, I decided to prepare myself for this first-time experience. I reasoned that if I showed up without drinking *at all*, I'd get myself into trouble or not know what I was doing. So, during my second semester of college, I chose to have my first drink.

I recall taking pulls of Fleischmann's Vodka like it was water. Then, I remember feeling tingly, the room spinning, and then, nothing at all. That was the beginning of my underage drinking experience.

Those next few years in college were a ton of fun. But I wasn't becoming who I truly wanted to be. I was raised to make better choices and be careful about who I surrounded myself with. But I still indulged in the temptation of partying and having fun above all else. Don't get me wrong: I enjoyed that period of time and made many new friends. The cost was that I made many poor choices and started many bad habits

For example, I didn't set aside time to read. The only thing I would read was the campus newspaper, and that was only to follow the names of students who would get busted for underage drinking or doing something stupid during the weekend. One of my buddies, a massive guy from the football team, had one of the best stories I ever read:

The campus newspaper reported that a college freshman dropped an unopened can of beer and it rolled under a vending machine. He had trouble reaching it, so he got creative.

You can probably guess that he was wasted and so, naturally, he decided that the *best* way to get behind the vending machine was to crawl on top and reach down behind it to grab his all-important beer. It makes you wonder how great that beer must've been; maybe it was an imported brand? After failing to reach it, he decided to dive down behind the machine headfirst. I mean, talk about commitment. Needless to say, he got stuck. And the story spread all over campus.

Stories like this remind me about who we are surrounded by in college. It's not always an uplifting reminder.

Most students develop these bad habits in college and never get the most out of their education. In fact, 60 percent of college freshman do not graduate in four years, according to *College Planning Partnerships*:

> *"Every fall approximately one million high school graduates begin their undergraduate careers at four-year colleges and universities in anticipation of earning a bachelor's degree.*
>
> *Fewer than four in 10 students graduate in four years, while just about six in 10 graduate in six years, according to a new report by The Education Trust, a non-profit organization based in Washington, D.C.*
>
> *'Too many students – far too many students – who start college never finish. The raw numbers are staggering. Fewer than four in 10 will graduate in four years,' Kevin Carey wrote in a recent report entitled, 'One Step from the Finish Line.'"*[12]

This is sad; and the main two reasons for this sad reality are too much partying and not enough money. For the ones who do graduate, many return to live with mom and dad after graduation. These individuals are called the "boomerang kids." The parents send them off to college and then they come right back after graduating.

Many students graduate with a diploma but don't walk away prepared to live life.

This is why young people, including some I'm sure you know, need *Daily Life University*.

After reading this course, you should understand the importance of growing as a young person and preparing for your future. Whether at work or in school, you must be developing yourself if you want to break away from the mediocre majority.

In the next course, you'll learn why most people won't implement The *Daily Life University* principles. And you'll have to decide if you want to be like most people.

Course 4 Assignment

1. Watch this funny YouTube video from "EveRy" University: https://youtu.be/T24DPU-hkJM. [13]

COURSE 5

The Majority Wants You

In this course, you'll learn how to not be like "most people." You'll realize most people are not living a happy and successful life. But there is good news:

Your entire life changes the moment you decide *not to be mediocre.*

Everything you need to make your dreams a reality is already within you. *This is important.* You don't have to settle and be miserable like the people you see around you. Yet 95 percent of those people are not living the life they truly want. They didn't grow up hoping to one day hate their job, to have tens of thousands of dollars of debt, or to struggle in relationships.

We all have this fantastic birthright to live – yet we face a challenge when we choose to live greatly.

What does the average person do to stay mediocre? They follow the crowd. They take advice from the wrong people. They take their parents' and professors' words as absolute truth.

But if you want to be successful and happy, you must go against the current – the current of the mediocre majority. Even though you exist as part of the same society, you don't want to just be another "cog in the system," as author Seth Godin describes in his book *Linchpin: Are You Indispensable?*[14]

The 5 Causes of Mediocrity

1. Lacking Purpose & Clarity

As humans, we need a compelling "why" to commit to doing something. We need something that motivates us, regardless of our surroundings. Simon Sinek, author *Start with Why*, writes:

> **You need a core belief that drives you to do what you do. This is your WHY.** [15]

If you don't have a reason for why you work and live, you won't have an end goal to visualize when the going gets tough. All of us are co-existing and trying to survive. If you are self-employed and your only reason for new projects is to make money, you can't possibly sustain motivation. If you have one good week and have enough money, why would you work the next week?

After you define your compelling "why", you need to clarify what stops you. Why are you part of the mediocre majority? What holds you back? Maybe it's accountability, or a lack of belief in your abilities, or even a bad habit such as making excuses. The reasons are endless, but it's your job to figure out what they are. Once you know what's stopping you, you can handle it.

Finally, you must figure out what habits you need to create and live, to further embody your purpose on a daily basis.

Good daily habits will carry you to great heights. Each day you'll need to work on what's holding you back from getting to where you want to be. It will be a daily grind because it's a long process, but you can do it.

Remember to focus on progress, not perfection.

2. Isolating Instances

You may think that doing that *one* thing that *one* time won't affect your life.

After all, eating the donut only affects you on that one day – right? Hitting the snooze button only affects you only on that morning – doesn't it? Failing to budget your money once doesn't *really* affect your long-term financial habits – does it?

It's easy to think that just one small mistake today – eating that donut, sleeping in, or spending outside the budget – is isolated from what happens tomorrow. However, we use this "just one time" excuse every day! A daily bad habit slowly but surely adds up.

How you do one thing in life is how you do *everything* in life.

You want to do what's right, not what's easy.

Those who only do what they feel like never do much. They lack self-discipline. And as these small decisions add up, you move further away from your dream life.

3. Rear-View Mirror Syndrome

Rear-view mirror syndrome is a limiting belief based on what's happened in the past. It's easy to look at the past and mentally convince yourself that the outcome of *one* situation will always be the outcome of *similar* situations.

You have to be willing to choose to be different from your past.

All of us are products of our past but none of us have to be prisoners of our past.

Believe in your potential and never judge it based on your past. To gain confidence, you can invest in personal development. **Your level of success will never be greater than your level of personal development.** You must improve in order to have your world improve. I strongly recommend scheduling time every day for personal development.

4. Lack of Commitment

Are you wholly committed to your goals? Are you ready to achieve them? Have you told others in order to hold yourself accountable?

Your willpower is strongest in the morning. Work on completing the most demanding tasks right away because once it's time to eat dinner, it's much more difficult to keep your motivation.

5. Lack of Urgency

Most people live with a "someday" mindset:

> "Someday, I'll ask her out. Someday I'll start that diet. Someday I'll start that workout. Someday I'll study for that test. Someday I'll start waking up earlier. Someday I'll start reading that book I bought two years ago. Someday I'll stop smoking or drinking. Someday I'll apply for a new job. Someday I'll treat my significant other better. Someday I'll start telling people close to me that I love them."

Sound familiar?

These statements are why so many people stay in the mediocre majority. It's the choice to never do today what you plan on doing someday that keeps you there. The truth is, you don't want to wake up 20 years from now and ask yourself, "What the heck happened?"

That is why this book is so important. To avoid falling into this rut, you need to become a student of life. You need to continually study success and improve yourself. By adapting the principles of **Daily Life University**, you will resist becoming a member of the mediocre majority. But you need to develop self-discipline and commit to daily improvements.

Your life is created through your habits. Commit to building one good habit for 30 days. After 30 days, your habit should be ingrained enough that you can move on to building your next habit. Mentally prepare yourself to take on this challenge for *at least* one month.

Think about New Year's resolutions: 95 percent of people give up within the first week. How do I know this? I watch fewer and fewer people come to the gym each day during the month of January!

Your goal should be to develop a new success habit *every month*. Accept that your 30-day goal will be developed in phases:

Phase 1

In the first 10 days of a new habit, your body will reject it. Your mind and body will do everything they can to get you to stop. You could call this "hell week." It is challenging and you'll want to give up every single day.

Phase 2

During days 11-20, you'll experience resistance. It will be uncomfortable – but not nearly as challenging as those first 10 days, because your mind and body are getting used to the habit. But it's still not "normal."

Phase 3

Finally, it's during days 21-30 when most people mess up. They think they did the 21-day habit and can now let down their guard – but that's not the case. The last 10 days are where you become unstoppable. Most people lose momentum and even take some days off. But all it takes is a few days of slacking and you are back at square one.

Live your life in 30-day challenges.

Imagine yourself one year from today if you developed 12 habits you didn't think you'd ever have. How would your life look today if you had implemented those 12 habits last year? How would you feel right now? That's how you'll feel a year from now if you start this challenge.

With this course, you understood the importance of doing things differently than most people. You are now mentally prepared for what it's going to be like to break away from the mediocre majority.

Now it's time to break it down even further. In the next course, you will realize the impact of your social groups. You will see the importance of choosing the people you spend the *most* time with. Your friends may have more of an effect on your future than your parents and education – combined!

Course 5 Assignments

1. Write down the 12 new habits you'd like to have this time next year:

   1. _____

   2. _____

   3. _____

   4. _____

   5. _____

   6. _____

   7. _____

   8. _____

   9. _____

10. _____

11. _____

12. _____

2. Now commit to one habit on the first day of each month for the next 12 months.

3. Write a list of 10 reasons why you don't want to be mediocre:

   1. _____

   2. _____

   3. _____

   4. _____

   5. _____

   6. _____

   7. _____

   8. _____

   9. _____

   10. _____

COURSE 6

Who is in Your Class of Life?

In this lesson, you will understand who is in your "class of life" and the impact these people have on you. You'll also discover how you can upgrade your "class" – starting right now.

Proverbs 27:17 (NLT) states: "*As iron sharpens iron, so a friend sharpens a friend.*" [16]

I learned a long time ago the importance of surrounding myself with great people when I started attending work conferences. I learned that I become the average of the five people I spend the most time with. If you are hanging out with five negative people who always complain, guess how much complaining you'll be doing? If you are hanging out with five unhealthy people who are out of shape and lack motivation, guess how often you'll go to the gym? If you are hanging out with five people who can never keep a job, guess how excited you'll be to go to work? If you are hanging out with five people who love to party and stay out till 2:00 a.m., guess what your bedtime will be?

Here's the good news: You can *choose* your social groups and who you spend the most time with. For example, if you're looking to improve your GPA, find five people who study diligently and already have a high GPA. If you're looking to get fit and healthy to attract someone special, look for five people in the gym and ask them about their good habits. If you're looking to have a great relationship with your significant other, find five people who have successful relationships in their lives.

Success leaves clues. Successful, wealthy, happy, and smart people make different choices than the mediocre majority. By spending time around successful people, you will naturally learn new habits and begin applying them in your own life. On the other hand, if you're hanging out with five unsuccessful people, you will find yourself observing and applying bad habits that are not doing you any favors.

How do you go about finding the right people? There are many opportunities to meet successful people and enhance your network. There are also great books that can teach you how to develop people skills and networking abilities. Here are some examples of actions you can take:

- Join your local Toastmasters group. You can develop your presentation skills while meeting other people interested in improving themselves.

- Join YOUR Chamber of Commerce. You'll learn about your city while making great connections with business leaders.

- Join a young professionals network. For example, in Appleton, WI, there is a group called "Pulse". This group is filled with professional people in their 20s and 30s, with similar hard-working mentalities.

- Join a networking group such as Business Network International (BNI). These groups provide opportunities for professionals to get together and share best practices as well as sales leads.

- Join a class at the gym. Typically, gym classes are filled with health-conscious, positive people.

In this course, you learned how your social group influences you. You also learned how to elevate your circle of influence. In the next course, you'll realize the mental ruts that make you feel like you are constantly chasing happiness, and never truly finding it.

Course 6 Assignments

1. Write the names of the five people you spend the most time with:

    1. _____

    2. _____

    3. _____

    4. _____

    5. _____

2. Analyze each person and rank him or her on a scale of 1 to 10 (1 being low, 10 being high) in each of these areas *(see example)*:

	#1	#2	#3	#4	#5	Average
Finances	___	___	___	___	___	_____
Fitness	___	___	___	___	___	_____
Happiness	___	___	___	___	___	_____
Relationships	___	___	___	___	___	_____
Positivity	___	___	___	___	___	_____
Making choices	___	___	___	___	___	_____
Integrity	___	___	___	___	___	_____

Overall average: _____

	DJ	Vern	Josh	Lizz	Alex	Total	Average
Finances	5	6	2	8	5	26	5.2
Fitness	8	6	5	6	6	31	6.2
Happiness	1	4	8	7	2	22	4.4
Relationships	3	9	4	5	6	27	5.4
Positivity	1	5	3	9	7	25	5
Making Choices	5	5	7	8	5	30	6
Integrity	3	7	7	5	8	30	6

Overall average: 5.5

3. Next, calculate the average score of each "area", based on the five people you spent the most time with. Finally, calculate the overall average of of the last column.

I just did this exercise with one of my life-coaching clients. Based on the numbers he rated his friends, he is living a life that ranks at 6.2. I asked him if he wanted to live at that level of success. He, of course, said, "No way!"

We all want to live a life that scores a 10 or above but if we surround ourselves with the wrong people, it'll be nearly impossible to get there. So I challenge you to really analyze the people you spend time with, and start spending less time with those who do not bring your life much value.

4. Rank yourself in each area, and circle the area that you would like to elevate the fastest.

5. Pick five people you'd like to spend more time with, especially considering who could help you improve in the area you circled in #4.

     1. _____

     2. _____

     3. _____

     4. _____

     5. _____

6. Shoot each of these people a quick text or email asking to get together for coffee or a 15-minute phone chat. Successful people love sharing what they're doing! Here's an example of an email you could send:

     Hi Jim,

     This is out of the blue but I could use some help. I have really admired _____ about you. I'd love to get some time with you to learn about what you're doing to succeed with_____. I would really appreciate it. It could be a 15-

minute phone call or grabbing a quick coffee. I know you're probably really busy; however, it would mean a lot to me. What does your schedule look like this week?

Have a great day,

Jason

COURSE 7

Happiness Myths We All Believe

This lesson is designed to show you how to become happier. You will also uncover myths about what most people believe brings them happiness.

As you grow and mature, you will spend a lot of time trying to understand what actually brings happiness. Is it material possessions, being popular, or getting the next pay raise at work? Is it all of the above? Or is there more?

Unfortunately, happiness is not related to any of those things. Think about the last time you received a pay raise at work. You may have been excited in the moment but, within hours, days, or even weeks, you were once again stressing about money and wishing you had more. Consider the last time you felt cool and popular. Once the circumstances changed, did you still feel insecure when you were by yourself? Or remember the day you bought a brand new car. Does that feeling still exist or have you gotten used to it now and envy someone who has the newer model?

Consider the diagram from Tony Hsieh's book, *Delivering Happiness*. It shows that all of us are striving for things that make us happy.[17]

Delivering Happiness: Ultimately, we all want to be happy. [17]

Tony Hsieh, the author of *Delivering Happiness*, is also the founder and

CEO of Zappos. His hugely successful company has an amazing culture and most of Tony's employees are truly happy at work. His book is a great read that I recommend to anyone.

In the book, Tony talks about the three different levels of happiness. According to his research and experiences with hundreds of customers and employees, the highest level of lasting happiness is giving back and making an impact.[17]

Tony illustrates these three types of happiness:

Rock Star, Flow, and Higher Purpose happiness.[17]

Giving to someone makes you feel much better than receiving something. Helping someone and taking time out of your day to impact his or her life can make you feel better about yourself. When you're living for a higher purpose than just yourself, you'll have a better outlook on life.

Another amazing book is Robin Sharma's *The Monk Who Sold His Ferrari*. This is one of my favorite books. It's about a famous and rich lawyer who had a heart attack, due to the fact that he was constantly stressed and lived a very unhealthy life. So, he decided to sell his Ferrari and go live with a group of monks, where he learned about peace and happiness. Most importantly, he learned that the chase for material possessions and money does not bring you lasting happiness. [18]

Most of us act very selfishly. We constantly want more and more. In the United States, we chase material possessions and higher incomes. We put pressure on ourselves to appear cool and successful to our friends. A quote by Dave Ramsey, a financial guru, describes this pandemic:

"We buy things we don't need with money we don't have to impress people we don't know." [19]

In *Off Balance*, best-selling author Matthew Kelly writes how, sometimes, you will need to devote more time and energy into your work *or* your family life. Expecting to do both successfully is just not feasible. [20]

Yes, there will be times you will have to put more energy and time into work. You're probably under the impression that the more energy you apply at work, the happier you will become. But this narrow view is chasing false hope.

Here's a story from Matthew Kelly's book:

Once upon a time there was an investment banker. He lived in New York City, was phenomenally successful, and made a ton of money.

But his life was busy, noisy, and very stressful.

So, once a year, he would leave the city and go down to a small coastal village in Mexico. For two weeks he would rest, relax, and allow himself to be rejuvenated.

One day, he was standing on the pier just before lunch, looking out to sea, when he noticed a small fishing boat coming in to dock. He thought this was a little strange, because most of the fishermen used to stay out late in to the afternoon so they could catch as many fish as possible, before coming in and preparing the fish for market.

Curiosity overcame him. So, he walked over to where the fishing boat was about to dock. Looking into the boat, he saw just one fisherman and several large yellowfin tuna.

"How long did it take you to catch those fish?" he said to the fisherman.

"Not very long," the fisherman replied with a smile.

"Is there something wrong with your boat?" the American asked.

"Oh, no," the fisherman said. "In thirteen years I have never had a problem with the boat."

The American was a little perplexed, so he asked the fisherman, "Why don't you stay out there longer and catch more fish?"

The fisherman smiled again and said, "This is plenty here for my family right now. Some of the fish we can eat, and the others we can sell or trade for the other things we need."

"But it's not even lunchtime. What do you do with the rest of your time?"

"In the morning," the fisherman explained, "I like to sleep late. When I wake I fish a little, mostly just for the pleasure of fishing. In the afternoon I play with my children and take siesta with my wife. In the evenings I have dinner with my family. And then, when my children are sleeping, I stroll into the village, where I sip wine and play guitar with my friends."

The American scoffed and said, "I'm a Harvard MBA and I can help you."

The fisherman was a little skeptical, but nonetheless he obliged and asked, "How?"

"You should fish longer every day," the American counseled, "late into the afternoon. This way you will catch more fish and make more money, and you can buy a bigger boat. With the bigger boat you will catch even more fish, make even more money, and then you can buy another boat and hire another man to work the second boat."

"But what then?" the fisherman asked.

"Before too long, you can cut out the middleman, sell your fish direct to the cannery, and make more money. As your fleet of boats continues to expand, you can build your own cannery. And before you know it, you'll be able to leave this small coastal village, move to Mexico City, and manage your expanding enterprise."

"But what then?" the fisherman persisted.

"Well then, you can begin to ship your fish to different parts of the world. Down into Asia and Australia and up into North America. And as demand grows for your fish, you can leave Mexico City, move to Los Angeles, open a distribution plant there, and begin to ship

your fish to Europe and every corner of the globe."

"But what then?" the fisherman asked again.

The American continued, "By then your business will be one of the great ventures of the industry. You can move to New York City and manage your empire from the epicenter of the business world."

"How long will all this take?" the fisherman asked.

"Twenty-five, maybe thirty years," the banker explained.

"But what will I do then?" the fisherman asked.

The American's eyes lit up like a Christmas tree. "That's the best part," he said. "When the time is just right, you can go down to Wall Street, list your business as a public company, offer an IPO, and make millions and millions of dollars."

"Millions?" the fisherman asked.

"More money than you ever dreamed you could earn in ten lifetimes," the American explained.

"But what then?" the fisherman asked.

The American did not know what to say. He had reached his climax. He was stumped. But then a thought crossed his mind and triggered an idea, and he turned once more to the fisherman and spoke.

"Well then, you could move to a small coastal village. . . You could sleep late. . . You could fish just for the pleasure of fishing. . . In the afternoons, you could take siesta with your wife. . . In the evenings, you could have dinner with your family . . . and then you could stroll into the village and sip wine and play guitar and sing songs with your friends. . ."[20]

The point of this story is that fisherman was already living his dream.

So, what is stopping your happiness? You may think, "I will be happy *when...*" But you can choose to be happy right now with what you have.

There's a poster that hangs in my office that states, *"Happiness is NOT a destination, it is a way of LIFE."*

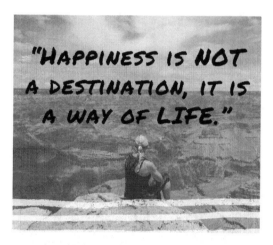

True happiness is a way of life. You can be happy right now in your current situation. You need to make the most of what you have. Do your best to make progress and give back to others. As you do that, you'll improve your happiness in life.

The next course may be the most impactful course in this whole book. It describes the realization I had years ago that took my life to a level I only dreamed of until that moment.

Course 7 Assignments

1. What are three false hopes you believe will make you happy?

    1. _____
    2. _____
    3. _____

2. What are three blessings that *should* appreciate each day?

    1. _____
    2. _____
    3. _____

3. Watch the movie, Hector and the Pursuit of Happiness.

PART 2

BECOMING A STUDENT OF LIFE TO
CONQUER THE PASSION SLUMP

COURSE 8.1

Take on Your Day with Morning Routines

In this lesson, you'll learn about the importance of a morning routine.

The foundation of this idea comes from Hal Elrod and his book, *The Miracle Morning*. [22] Hal is one of my greatest mentors and his book was one of the catalysts for taking my life to the next level. Course 8 is dedicated to Hal's philosophy and the worldwide movement created by the *Miracle Morning*. I encourage you to buy your own copy; however, you're about to get the **Daily Life University** take on what it's all about.

It all started in November 2012. I read *The Miracle Morning* – and everything in my life changed.

I had always heard about the benefits of getting the day started early, but I never made a commitment to do it. So I started by waking up at least one hour earlier than normal. And before I knew it, I started waking up because I *wanted* to, not because I *had* to.

Most people wake up because they have to. They wake up at the very last minute after hitting the snooze button five times. They rush and frantically try to get everything done before they have to start their day. As you can imagine, this does not give them a successful start to the day.

How you start your morning determines the direction of your day.

This of each morning as the rudder of a boat. A rudder's direction guides the boat just like a morning's direction guides the day. Starting your day on the wrong foot carries into every part of that day. But when you start your day energized and excited to be awake – when the rudder points where you truly want it to take you – your whole day is easier and you achieve *more* success with *less* effort.

But why the *morning*? Couldn't we just dedicate extra time at the end of each day, when we're already awake?

The point of a morning routine is simple. You already know many habits you could implement to become more successful – but you don't do them. Why? It's because you are too busy and too tired to add these habits into your daily routine.

Life isn't always a walk in the park; it takes energy and effort. Once it gets dark, I start winding down for the evening. Any ambitions I had in the morning – and even the night before – to accomplish various tasks will not actually happen as my body and mind are winding down. My emotions and mental Acuity are not nearly as strong as they were in the morning.

Since reading the *The Miracle Morning*, I love starting my day off knowing I will be successful. And I don't have to worry about the when and where the rest of my day because all of it happens in the morning.

In college, I remember trying to do homework, work out, and accomplish important tasks at night. What always happened is something you can relate to: I didn't *feel like* doing any of those things!

I was so worried about fitting everything into my day that the majority of my time and energy went into thinking about how I had to go to the gym and exercise later; how I needed to get all my homework completed before tomorrow's deadline; how I had to find time to work on my book. I was distracted by all of these future "to-do's" so everything I did throughout the day suffered.

Today, I feel so empowered knowing that by 8:00 a.m., I will have accomplished all of the important tasks I need to be happy and grounded. I'm ready for my day.

Your morning routine *can* be different than what it is right now. The tips and suggestions you're about to discover have helped thousands of people. But remember, your morning routine is yours to make. It can be five minutes or two hours.

Establishing a morning routine can be an especially daunting change for young people. Waking up early is the last choice many want to make after staying up late checking social media, watching TV, or playing video games with friends. *But your morning can start anytime.* For example, if you normally wake up at 10:00 a.m., your morning routine can start at 9:00 a.m. Or if your workday begins at 8:00 a.m. and you normally wake up at 7:00 a.m., you can start your morning routine at 6:00 a.m. What's important is not *what time* you wake up, but that you wake up *earlier than you have to.*

As you read this, you might be thinking, "I don't like mornings and I'm not a morning person."

Most people aren't naturally morning people. It's just a choice you have to make.

I don't believe there are ways in which we are "wired." Rather, I believe there are mentalities we choose to operate from. There are certainly external influences that play a part in creating those mentalities, such as your upbringing and surroundings. But I can tell you I was never a morning person. Nonetheless, I still woke up at 8:00 a.m. for classes and 6:00 a.m. for football practice – yet I was far from an early bird.

After reading *The Miracle Morning*, I began waking up at 5:00 a.m. every day. It became very important to me to dedicate a couple hours towards my personal growth. It made me feel amazing all day – and it truly changed my life.

Course 8.1 Assignments

1. Read this **Daily Life University** article on the *Miracle Morning* and watch the 10-minute video: https://dailylifeuniversity.wordpress.com/the-miracle-morning/ [23]

2. Order Hal Elrod's book, *The Miracle Morning*, [22] and start reading it once you finish this one.

COURSE 8.2

The Miracle Morning

In *The Miracle Morning*, Hal mentions what he's dubbed Life SAVERS. [22]

It stands for:

Silence

Affirmations

Visualization

Exercise

Reading

Scribing

Every morning, successful people use these six great practices to prepare for the day ahead. I'll break each one down.

Silence

Today's world is so busy. People are constantly moving, thinking, and watching. Rarely do people give themselves a break. And when they try to relax, they fill their minds with TV and social media.

Your mind is a powerful tool – but if you don't give your brain time to rest and recover, it can't operate at full capacity. Many young people are stressed beyond capacity because they don't give themselves the time to let their minds be at peace.

Every morning, my peacetime is 5 to 10 minutes of prayer and meditation. It's amazing what ideas and solutions I come up with when I give myself time to just relax. For those of you who are religious, there is a powerful movie on prayer called *War Room*. [24]

Whether or not you consider yourself religious, you can download an app called Headspace. [25] This simple and popular app is very easy to use for beginners, and currently offers a free trial period. Headspace really helped me understand meditation in a simple and fun way – and Andy, the app's founder, has a really cool British accent!

Young people's minds are worn out from information and technology overload that even taking a few minutes to breathe and be silent can help them stay focused on the rest of their day.

Affirmations

Affirmations may seem odd to most people. The truth is they can really help your mentality.

Many young people are insecure because they don't believe in themselves. They want to be like everybody else. They want to be cool and they want to be loved, but do not always feel that way.

That's how affirmations can help. They fill your mind with *positive expectancy.* You are programming your brain for success. Tony Robbins describes these as "incantations." [26] Basically, affirmations are a mission you speak to yourself that re-programs your mind for the day. Whether you speak them or listen to a recording on your phone of yourself saying them, their effects are very powerful.

If you've read the book *The Secret* by Rhonda Byrne, you know the importance of filling your mind with positive expectancy in order to bring success and happiness. When you believe and expect something, you subconsciously move towards it. As you remind your mind of your mission, it'll pick up on opportunities and ideas that align with that mission. [27]

Take five minutes in the morning to read your affirmation to direct your day towards success. It's crazy to look back at my affirmations from 2015 and realize how much I was speaking into reality as most of these are just who I am now!

Here were my affirmations from 2015:

Life Purpose: *My mission is to utilize my communication skills, life experiences, and genuine love for people to connect with and coach others in such a way that I am able to have a powerful and lasting impact on their lives. When I am gone, I do not want to be remembered for my personal accomplishments, but for the value I added and the difference I made in the lives of the people I touched. I know that I can only expect of others what I display myself, so to fulfill my mission I must be selfless, practice daily discipline, act with integrity, treat all people with love and respect, pursue my goals with extraordinary effort and unwavering faith, place a never ending importance on personal growth, follow God, and show daily gratitude for my life and the people in it.*

God: *God loves me unconditionally. God has a plan for my life and is guiding me every step of the way. I would have nothing without God* blessing me. I will do everything as if I am doing it for him. All things are possible when I actively seek God. (Philippians 4:13)

Gratitude*: Experience gratitude in every moment, in everything I do. I am blessed to have the life, freedoms, and support around me that God has blessed me with.*

Overcoming Fear & Worry*: Only think positive, self-affirming, and confidence inspiring thoughts. There is literally nothing to fear or worry about, because I cannot fail, only learn and grow.*

Protecting My Time*: Every minute is worth $1 to me. I will use my time wisely by focusing on the top 20 percent of result producing activities. I do not have time for distractions and I will interrupt interruptions by sticking to my schedule. I will delegate what I do not have time to do because others can accomplish it just as well.*

Success at Work*: I will stop letting my limiting beliefs get in the way of my success. Through Servant Leadership, I will attract and retain leaders by holding them accountable to their best. I will be a tough coach on my people, through Crucial Conversations, because they not only NEED it, but they WANT it. By helping others accomplish their DREAMS, I will be able to accomplish mine.*

Authenticity/Self Confidence*: Give up being perfect for being authentic. I won't make everyone happy. Some will judge me and criticize me, while most will praise me, honor me, respect me, support me, and pray for my continued success. Everyone who truly knows me, LOVES me because of the value I share. I will portray this in my physiology and voice tone. What I say matters and I do not need to validate my leadership.*

Developing People*: When I am with that person, he or she is the most important (and the only) person in the room. (Active Listening) Make* every person feel like a million bucks, no matter who they are! *(Appreciative Leadership – leaving a positive wake)*. Do this TODAY with EVERY person I come in contact with.

Rest & Relaxation*: Taking moments to step back and recharge are crucial for my happiness, health, and success. Moments away from work provide me with new perspective and ideas by removing me from my day-to-day routine, environment, and allow me to share carefree timelessness with family and friends.*

Being Present/Journaling*: I will invest time in reflection, gaining a deeper perspective by asking questions like: What am I doing well that I need to acknowledge myself for? What can I be doing better? What are 3 things I'm grateful for today? What 3 things did I learn today?*

Circle of Influence*: I will surround myself with people who challenge me and bring me up. People who truly care about me and will hold me accountable. I will surround myself with positive, Christian, successful, healthy, hard-working, and loving people.*

My Health*: I am committed to following the Tony Robbins Health Plan. I know by doing so, I will feel great, look amazing, and have an abundance of energy. Even at times when I am tempted, I will resist because that short period of pleasure will conflict with the feeling of long-term happiness.*

Financial Abundance*: My commitment in 2015 is to PROFIT over $100,000 – on my way to $300,000/year. The more money I earn/save, the greater the impact I can have on others. I am just as capable of becoming extraordinary wealthy as any other person. Also, I am committed to following the "The Total Money Makeover" and living below my means. I know that reaching this level of personal income will allow me to provide for my family, enjoy life to the fullest, travel, prepare* for retirement, and give back to people less fortunate than myself. Every day I am getting more confident in my finances.

Attracting My Life Partner: *I will meet, attract, and eventually marry a woman who is kind, loving, fun, easy-going, open-minded, positive, enthusiastic, trustworthy, healthy, appreciative, and forgiving (Proverbs 31). We will connect mentally, physically, emotionally, and spiritually. We will share strong values and morals. She will fit in with my friends and family. Considering that we will be fighting life's battles together, she will be able to handle adversity well. I understand that in order to attract her, it is my responsibility to display the same qualities that I desire in her. I will always love and appreciate her for who she is.*

Sexual Pureness: *I will not have sex before marriage from this day out. I know that God intended sex for marriage to make a man and a woman one. By doing this, I will be saving my mind and soul for who God has intended for me. I know that if I look at pornography or have sex that it will be detrimental to the way I view women and my future relationships.*

My Affirmations: *The words I have spoken to myself in the paragraphs above come straight from my heart. They are important and should never be taken lightly. I am human and I make mistakes, which is why it is critical to always remind myself of my vision and who I want to be. I understand that reaching this level of professional excellence will not be easy and that I will face many challenges along the way, but I will not let any obstacle or adversity derail me. I will always choose to value my goals and my vision over my excuses. I will read these affirmations each morning. I will let the words influence and direct me each time, as I continue to pursue my life's ambitions.*

My Best Year Ever: *I acknowledge that I am just as worthy, deserving, and capable of creating extraordinary success and achieving all my goals* *in 2015 as any other person on earth, and that the only thing that separates me from those at the top is my level of commitment. I must get out of my comfort zone, take risks, and take action. So, I am 100 percent committed to making this my best year ever, and I know that to do this, I must be willing to commit at a level that I have never committed before. I am no longer willing to settle for less than I am truly capable of. If I am to create my best life, I cannot wait for someday, or some year in the future. I must do it NOW. So, stop reading and make it happen.*

You can also check out this video of my affirmations: https://dailylifeuniversity.wordpress.com/the-miracle-morning/daily-affirmations-re-program-your-brain/. [28]

Visualization

Visualization may seem similar to affirmations but it is very different. Affirmations are *speaking* what you want, whereas visualization is *picturing* your success. There's a reason why top athletes visualize themselves succeeding before the big shot or field goal. When you listen to an athlete talk after the game, they had a firm belief that they were going to make the game-winning shot or game-winning field goal. Talented athletes are also human!

It's very important to visualize yourself being successful and accomplishing what you want, because subconsciously, your brain will begin to work towards that goal.

To have a better chance of asking the girl across the room on a date, visualize yourself walking up to her with confidence and sweeping her off her feet with your winning personality. When you do this, it won't guarantee a date, but it will help you be more confident when you actually take that step.

But visualizing success is the opposite of what most people do. Most worry about the negative and worst-case scenarios.

In the example above, most guys may visualize the girl throwing a drink in his face, rejecting him, and everyone around him staring as it happens. But how often does that really happen? It probably won't happen – assuming he is respectful and honest. But self-doubt eliminates any confidence while he goes in for the introduction.

If you want to ace that final, ask that cute man or woman out for coffee, become healthy and fit, or even make that game-winning shot, start visualizing yourself doing those things and you'll be amazed at how much success you will experience.

Exercise

There are countless websites and books about health, exercise and fitness. You don't need the details about how to exercise, because the information is already available. What's important is learning how easy it can be to commit to doing it every morning.

Many people fail to commit to daily exercise. They try to find the best diet or the best workout plan instead of just doing *something*. There's nothing more draining than talking about working out, thinking about working out, but not actually working out. How do you change that?

Exercise is really important to my morning routine – it gets my blood pumping along with countless other benefits.

Exercise wakes me up. Believe it or not, I don't always jump out of bed excited for the day to begin. Naturally, my body is still in sleep mode, so I'll trick myself by just doing some light movements and twists to get the blood flowing. Then I follow that up with rebounding.

Rebounding on a mini, therapeutic trampoline is a really easy and healthy way to exercise the body. It strengthens your cells and organs, improves your circulation, and tones your muscles. For information on the benefits of rebounding, check out the brand I recommend: Pure Fun. [29]

After that, I always exercise for at least 30 minutes. It could be a run, going to the gym, or yoga. You don't have to commit to a strenuous two-hour workout and slam a protein shake afterwards to be fit. During college, I would go to the gym for two hours a day trying to build muscle to impress the ladies and feel good about myself. Although this helped me in sports, it wasn't necessary to stay fit and healthy. After retiring from football at UW-Whitewater, my exercise routine changed.

To have your best day, it's crucial to receive the health benefits that come from working up a sweat for at least 30 minutes. A healthy day starts with exercise to get your metabolism working. You'll also find it easier to stay fit when working out in the morning because the body starts burning fat earlier in the day.

Exercise is something we know we can benefit from. We just need to build the habit! So find the time to do it *early* because by the end of the day, you'll be less interested in working out and more interested in lounging on your couch.

Reading

Reading is crucial to starting your day on the right foot.

When I was in college, I rarely enjoyed reading. But once I learned about personal growth through my early days in Cutco, I became more open to the habit.

When I read something, I challenge myself to understand what I am learning from the book. I often highlight and making notes right on the pages. In *The Miracle Morning*, Hal writes that if a person consistently reads just 10 pages each day, he or she would read 18 200-page books every year. [22] This amazed me – I didn't even read 18 books during my five years at college!

"Ten pages a day?" I thought. "That's 15 minutes – well, 20 minutes since I'm a slow reader. I can spare 20 minutes of social media per day. I can spend 20 minutes less watching TV. And really, waking up 20 minutes earlier is not going to make me feel *that* tired. Showing up 20 minutes later won't ruin that party tonight." After getting into this habit of reading 10 pages a day, my personal growth was taken to a whole new level.

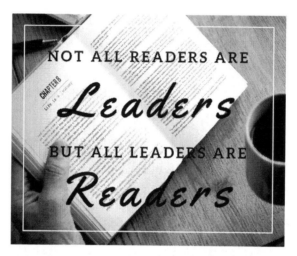

What's great about today's world is that we can learn anything from an expert by just picking up a book. There are many successful people in all areas of life who have shared their expertise, their secrets, and their hacks for achieving success.

In the past two years, I've read more books than in the first 25 years of my life. If you are just getting into personal growth, these are some of the best books you can start reading. It's part of *Daily Life University*'s "Powerful Monthly Book Club":

Read a Powerful Book Every Month:

January *The 15 Invaluable Laws of Growth* by John Maxwell [30]

February *The Enemies of Excellence* by Greg Salciccioli [31]

March *7 Habits of Highly Effective People* by Stephen Covey [32]

April *The Leader Who Had No Title* by Robin Sharma [33]

May *Taking Life Head On* by Hal Elrod [34]

June *The Miracle Morning* by Hal Elrod [22]

July *Delivering Happiness* by Tony Hsieh [35]

August *The Four Agreements* by Don Miguel Ruiz [36]

September *The Rhythm of Life* by Matthew Kelly [37]

October *Think and Grow Rich* by Napoleon Hill [38]

November *Dream Manager* by Matthew Kelly [40]

December *Total Money Makeover* by Dave Ramsey [19]

Today, my morning reading is flexible. I treat this as a time to grow rather than a time to complete a set number of pages. One morning I may read a book, the next I may listen to an audiobook, and on another, I may just watch an inspirational YouTube video. Whatever medium I choose, the point is to grow as a person.

Scribing

"Scribing" simply means journaling or writing down your thoughts. I used to think journaling was dumb and a waste of time. It reminded me of a middle school student writing in her diary about the boy she likes, but journaling – or scribing – is much more than that.

Journaling is an opportunity to gather your thoughts and highlight your wins for the day.

I've been journaling for over five years, and it's exciting to look back at the things I wrote. Through the years, I've noticed progress in areas I didn't realize were progressing until I saw the patterns in my journal.

Time flies quickly, and we that sometimes need to remember the greatest moments of our lives. I love looking back at the progress my wife and I have experienced Re-reading the journal entry from the day I first met her is especially special. As a business owner, I can also look back to see what I was thinking during the high and low times of my business and how my mentality has changed.

Analyzing your thoughts and feelings and reflecting on your journey is therapeutic and lets you reconnect with yourself. By taking the time to think about what you're grateful for on a daily basis, you start the day off *feeling* grateful. Every six months, dedicate time look back on all of the lessons you've learned. You'll be amazed. Patterns will emerge, and you'll see the choices you made during your wins as well as your frustrations.

I look at the big picture of the last six months and feel great about my accomplishments. But I also look for areas of opportunity. It's interesting to read about the same struggle week after week, and not realizing I'm repeating it until I read over it in my journal. I can make the adjustments necessary to grow and move forward in this area.

It only takes five minutes to journal. Yet those five-minute journaling sessions have been a great addition to my daily routine.

Assignment for Course 8.2

1. There is a product called "Five Minute Journal." Order it and use it to start your journaling habit: http://www.fiveminutejournal.com/. [41]

COURSE 8.3

Breakfast

The other benefit of a successful morning routine is waking up in time to have breakfast.

Newsflash: Breakfast is the most important meal of the day. But even though you may already know this, disciplining yourself to eat a good breakfast can be difficult.

When you wake up and supply your body with the right nutrients, not only will you look better, you'll actually feel better.

Every morning, I use my juicer to make a healthy and beneficial morning drink. I typically juice one apple, one orange, one lime, a couple carrots, one cucumber, a couple celery stalks, a piece of pineapple, and a little clove of ginger. There's no way I would have room in my stomach to eat all this, but I reap the benefits of the nutrients all day because I drink them instead. There are tons of benefits to juicing, such as weight loss and reducing your chance of disease.

Assignment for Course 8.3

1. To learn more about the benefits of juicing, watch *Fat, Sick, and Nearly Dead*.[42] You'll learn that the energy and health you'll get from drinking fruits and vegetables is a perfect way to kick-start your day.

COURSE 8.4

My Miracle Morning

Below, you'll find an hour-by-hour schedule of my miracle morning.

I printed this in color and laminated it, and then put a copy in my bathroom so I could look at it each morning and evening. I also hung it on my fridge so I could see it every time I ate. Looking at this schedule multiple times each day reminds me that sticking to my routine today is key to leading a successful tomorrow.

> "An extraordinary life is all about daily, continuous improvements in the areas that matter most." – Robin Sharma

The Night Before

9:30 p.m.	Read Evening Affirmations, Deep Breathing, & Prayer
10:00 p.m.	Go to bed

The Miracle Morning

4:45 a.m.	Wake up (alarm across the room, glass of water, rebound) [43]
5:00 a.m.	Silence/Deep Breathing
5:05 a.m.	Devotion/Prayer

5:15 a.m.	5 Minute Journal
5:20 a.m.	Read 10+ pages
5:40 a.m.	Read Affirmations
5:50 a.m.	Exercise
6:40 a.m.	Make Smoothie and Juice
7:00 a.m.	Get Ready
7:20 a.m.	Leave for work to CHANGE LIVES
7:45 a.m.	Plan out the day
8:00 a.m.	"Swallow the Frog" tackle toughest/most important tasks [44]

Keep these words in mind as you wrap up Course 8:

"Time is limited, so I will wake up every morning and know that I have one chance to live this day to the best of my ability, and string my days together into a life of success and happiness." – Jason Heinritz

Now that you know how important and easy it is to have a successful morning, this course should serve as your starting point for a changed life.

In the next course, you'll learn the one key to an amazing morning that has nothing to do with what you choose to do before 8:00 a.m.

Course 8 Assignments

1. Put together your own morning routine – make sure it excites you! The routine does not need to be perfect. However, as you practice, you'll make minor adjustments as you discover what does and doesn't work.

2. Order *The Miracle Morning* by Hal Elrod, [22] if you haven't already. It's part of the monthly book club, and will truly transform your morning routine.

COURSE 9

Your Day Begins the Night Before with a *Necessary Night*

Course 9 will let you in on the secret that will let you have a great morning, every morning. And it all starts with the night before.

After reading the last lesson, you understood the importance of having a morning routine. But if you have any kind of excuse for not being as productive in the morning, chances are it's because of your evening routine.

Here's the secret: Your morning actually starts the night before.

It's not always easy to maintain the ambition and drive you need to wake up early and practice personal growth, exercise, and work on homework. This is especially true when you're out late partying or watching TV; none of this really brings us any value. These activities do not mentally and physically prepare you for your productive morning.

To combat this, I came up with what I call the *Necessary Night*. All of us know we need to get a certain amount of sleep each night. But how much sleep do we actually need?

Shawn Stevenson wrote an amazing book called *Sleep Smarter*. [45] I'd like to share a few key points from the book:

Evening Routine

First, it's important to have an evening routine. We are creatures of habit. We need a good hour to wind down before we go to bed. Too many of us are playing video games, watching TV, and being too active right before going to bed. This causes our brains to stay turned on, which makes going to bed a struggle. But instituting an evening ritual helps our bodies to go to bed faster and easier. [45]

Second, Shawn recommends turning off all electronics at least one hour before bed. Our minds think it's still daytime due to all the blue light emanating from our devices, which keeps us awake. An increasing number of young people look tired, with bags under their eyes, because they're not getting enough quality sleep. This can be attributed to scrolling through social media until 1:00 or 2:00 a.m., so young people get only a few hours of sleep before class or work. [45]

Finally, to combat late night scrolling, Shawn recommends setting an evening alarm. This helps your body gets used to going to bed and waking up at regular times. Our bodies already know how much sleep is needed to feel good. The disconnect most people have is between wanting to get up at a certain time and failing to apply that desire to going to bed at a reasonable hour. [45]

Setting Your Alarm at Night

Your evening alarm is even more important than your morning alarm.

Many of us have trouble getting up but have no trouble hitting the snooze button. We feel tired – not because of how early it is, but because of our choices the evening before. We intend to go to bed but are distracted by momentary pleasures such as watching TV or scrolling through our social media accounts. We finally get to bed one or two hours later than originally planned. Inevitably, our morning routine is affected.

If you know you operate best on six or seven hours of sleep, plan ahead.

My evening alarm is set for 9:20 p.m. because I know that realistically, from the time it goes off, it will take me another 30 or 60 minutes to get to bed. That is, of course, if I don't succumb to the instant pleasure of scrolling through social media or emails before my eyes shut.

What time will you set your evening alarm for so that you'll wake up *when* you want to and live the life of your dreams?

To help you go to bed the right way, below are Hal Elrod's *Miracle Morning* bedtime affirmations. [22]

First: Clean Up!

I have completed all of my daily tasks necessary to prepare myself for The Miracle Morning tomorrow. I have thoughtfully created clarity for what time I am waking up and what I will do when I wake up. I am anticipating the morning with positive expectations because I am well aware of the benefits that will result in my life by choosing to live The Miracle Morning.

Second: Rest Up!

Going to bed tonight at ___ tonight and waking up at ___ gives me ___ hours of sleep. This is PLENTY; in fact, it is much more than I really need in order to perform at peak level tomorrow. I cannot allow myself to fall into the belief that sleeping more will somehow improve my life; in fact, it will be seriously detrimental to my stress level, finances, marriage, career, and lifestyle goals. My quality of life as I know it depends on waking up on time tomorrow.

Third: Wake Up!

I am waking up at _____ tomorrow morning. By doing so, I significantly increase the likelihood that I will achieve my goals this week, this month, this year or for my life. This includes all aspects of my life: lifestyle goals, income goals, family goals, relationship goals, and all of my other personal and professional goals. I am committed to waking up on time tomorrow, because I know that how I start my days determines how I create my life.

Regardless of what I dream about, how long it takes to fall asleep, or how tired or overwhelmed I feel right now, or how I feel when I wake up, I will energetically jump out of bed tomorrow at _____ and create my best life![22]

Before you set your evening alarm and print your evening affirmations, you need to know how much sleep you actually need.

The number of required hours of sleep varies between age groups and levels of health. When you are younger, you need more sleep because your body is developing and growing. WebMD states that adults can function on six hours of sleep. [46]

Though this is not a healthy routine on a daily basis, it's possible to function fine on six hours. There are examples of successful people – Tony Robbins, for example – who only sleep for four to five hours each night. Though it may sound extreme, if you follow someone like Tony, you'll realize how his healthy lifestyle and mental discipline allows him to get by with fewer hours spent recovering in bed.

To be at optimum health, however, you'll need closer to seven or eight hours of sleep. [46]

You've likely heard of REM sleep cycles and how important they are to a restful sleep. REM stands for rapid eye movement. Every 90 minutes, your body goes through one REM cycle. In order to allow the body to fully repair itself after a day of being active, it's very important to move into that state of REM. To ensure this happens, you can schedule your sleep based on 90-minute intervals. In other words, if you're going to sleep, sleep for six hours, seven-and-a-half hours, or nine hours. Sleeping for seven-and-a-half hours is ideal for most people. However, if you maintain a healthy lifestyle – exercising daily, eating well, and avoiding too much stress – you can do with fewer hours of sleep.

My goal is to get at least six hours of sleep every night. After six hours, I feel rested and have plenty of time to exercise *The Miracle Morning*. Usually, I sleep from 10:30 p.m. to 4:30 a.m. My evening alarm is set at 9:20 p.m. so I have a solid hour to wind down and prepare for the next day.

However, I recommend most people get 7.5 hours of sleep a night. Even though I often want to sleep in, I resist the temptation to stay in bed, because I'm passionate about my goals and my dreams. I am also prepared, thanks to my *Necessary Night* routine, which quickly helps me get over any resistance. As with everything else, it takes practice.

To enhance your quality of sleep, don't eat anything at least two hours before going to sleep. You'll read more about healthy eating in the next lesson, but for now, recognize that eating food and processing it is one of the most energy-intensive bodily processes. Since it takes the body a lot of energy to process the food you just consumed, there's no way it can shut down for the night and begin to recover.

My general rule of thumb is to not eat after 7:00 p.m. That way, I can go to bed around 10:00 p.m. and avoid tossing and turning while my body digests my late night snack. My body is fully ready to repair itself from the day while I get a great sleep. I also fall sleep much faster because I don't fill my body with excess energy.

Adding the *Necessary Night* to your routine is a simple choice that will set up your next morning for success in a massive way. Having discipline during your mornings and evenings is crucial to living an extraordinary life.

Still, it can be hard sustaining your motivation throughout the day. In the next course, you will learn the secret to staying energized and motivated throughout your day.

Course 9 Assignments

1. Set your evening alarm for one hour ahead of your bedtime. Doing this right now, while your mind is focused on success, will actually make it easier to turn it into a habit.

2. Print Hal Elrod's evening affirmations and post them in your bathroom or in your kitchen to make them easy to read before bed each night.

COURSE 10

How to Re-Fuel with an *Energizing Lunch*

In this course, you will learn how to stay motivated and stay on track while maintaining a busy schedule.

Do you feel like you don't have the time or energy to accomplish everything you want during the day? The solution is surprisingly simple and will not only keep you energized, but also enhance your efficiency throughout the second half of your day: Make sure you have an *Energizing Lunch*.

> *"Lunch is a critical time of the day for me. I need a mental and emotional break and time to recharge my energy for an effective afternoon."*
> – Greg Salciccioli, author of 7 Enemies of Excellence [31]

The *Energizing Lunch* is a concept presented by Greg Salciccioli in *7 Enemies of Excellence*. In his book, Greg talks about doing something in the middle of your day to recharge. [31]

One reason most people fail to have an *Energizing Lunch* is because of a perceived lack of time. Too often, people believe they are too busy to take a step back and recharge. In *The Seven Habits of Highly Effective People*, Stephen Covey describes the seventh habit as "sharpening the saw." He writes that it's important to take a step back in order to take many steps forward. His analogy involves a lumberjack cutting down a tree. If the lumberjack continues sawing without stopping to sharpen his saw, it will eventually become dull and his work will become much more difficult. To stay effective, the lumberjack has to stop to sharpen his saw in order to stay effective. Even though it may take time to sharpen the saw, the lumberjack will ultimately cut down the tree faster and with less effort by always having a sharp saw. [32]

IF I HAD FOUR HOURS TO CHOP DOWN A TREE, I'D SPEND THE FIRST TWO HOURS SHARPENING THE AXE

The same applies to your body and mind. Every so often, you have to stop what you're doing in order to stay sharp. All of us lead busy lives. We constantly consume information and perform activities but we rarely take a moment to recharge.

I know the power of an *Energizing Lunch* firsthand. For many years as a District Manager at Cutco, I would work right through my workday, failing to take a break and eat. And when I would take a lunch break, it would be a stressful experience that involved picking a restaurant, waiting in traffic, and then rushing to make sure I would be back in the office on time. It was too easy to avoid taking a break, especially when I was busy assisting fellow managers while trying to complete my own tasks on time. Since I was so occupied, I would forget to take 30 or 45 minutes to recharge.

But recharging halfway through your day is important. Working through lunch sets you up for a less efficient rest of the day. When you have a short timeframe for lunch in the midst of a stressful work or school day, eating barely nourishing (and often expensive) food simply drags you down. It's no wonder you can't stay motivated and energized for the second half of your day.

**Use your lunchtime as a way to energize
yourself to dominate the rest of your day.**

Three Components of an *Energizing Lunch*

Key components of an *Energizing Lunch* include eating healthy, taking time to relax with meditation and gratitude, getting the blood pumping with a walk or rebounding session, and, finally, looking at how you'll tackle the second half of your day.

When it comes to eating a healthy lunch, it's important to include fruit, salad greens, or smoothies. Otherwise, you'll find yourself craving a pick-me-up coffee or energy shot.

It's equally important to put your mind in a positive space. If you're having a stressful day, taking a break to meditate for 10 minutes – the Headspace app [25] you already read about in course 8.2 is perfect for this – can help tremendously. Another option is to think about what you're grateful for and what you're accomplishing today. On a busy morning, it's easy to feel overwhelmed and focus on the negative rather than the positive aspects of your day. This is the time to get into a space of gratitude and look at your wins. You'll feel much better about yourself and will be in a better place the rest of the day.

To maximize your *Energizing Lunch*, you need to get the body pumping. Your body is designed to move – but unfortunately, today's working environment makes it hard to move much throughout the day. Your energy and opinion of yourself will improve tremendously if you take just 10 minutes to rebound or take a brisk walk. The point is not to do anything strenuous and work up a sweat – just to get the blood pumping and your body will feel great.

Below is an example of my *Energizing Lunch* routine:

Energizing Lunch (30-45 minutes)

Bonus Tip: To never miss a lunch, set the alarm on your phone to display an inspirational quote five minutes before lunchtime.

15-25 minutes – Healthy, homemade lunch (salad, smoothie, fruit)
5-10 minutes – Moment of peace

- What am I grateful for?

- Meditation

- Affirmations

- Am I on track with my intentions today?

- What wins have I already had today?

5-10 minutes – Get the blood pumping

- Walk

- Do jumping jacks

- Rebound

- Deep breathing exercise

In this course, you learned how to use your lunch to work *for* you as opposed to *against* you. Next, you will learn about ***Daily Life University.*** If you think the miracle morning was life-changing, the next lesson will transform your mornings even further.

Course 10 Assignments

1. Create your own energizing lunch routine, print it, and try it at least once this week.

2. Download the Headspace app [25] and commit to the free trial.

COURSE 11

The *Daily Life University* Program – More Valuable Than a 4-Year Degree

Here it is: the lesson that enhances a concept that's already life-changing. Think of this lesson like having your first banana split sundae, only to realize you can put chocolate fudge all over it.

This is the daily program I've developed for you. I've been influenced by many of really smart and successful people, so I've taken their ideas and put my own spin on it.

We all need to have a daily routine. If we don't create daily habits, we will miss daily habits that keep us on track, and we won't be as successful as we want to be. Every day is important.

Because our life is made up of our days, so we need to live every day with intention.

I recently read a quote by John C. Maxwell: *"You'll never change your life until you change something you do daily. The secret of your success is found in your daily routine."*[47]

95

I came up with the concept for *Daily Life University* after spending 10 years with Cutco and learning about the value of personal growth. There are many areas to focus your personal growth efforts, but I have not seen a program that shows you how to put all of them together. After studying personal growth, I realized I didn't know what to do with the huge amount of information I'd accumulated over 10 years! So, I decided to implement all of it and find a way to make it work together. *Daily Life University* is the result after I took the seven most important principles of personal growth, and transformed them into a simple, weekly program for others to follow.

Here's the hard truth: If you are investing time into improving your finances but you aren't healthy or growing in your relationships, your money doesn't really matter. If you are healthy and on track to live well past 100 years, but don't have enough money, you can't really enjoy those extra years. If you don't have great relationships with family, friends, or your significant other, you have no one with whom to enjoy that money and time.

These concepts are further explained – with the help of really cool videos – on DailyLifeUniversity.com

I will next cover what I recommend for each day of the week. But it is up to you to dive into these topics more deeply. Each day could be a full book!

Each day of the week, according to the *Daily Life University* plan:

- Mentality Monday
- Grati-Tuesday
- Wellness Wednesday
- Thriving Relationships Thursday
- Financial Abundance Friday
- Select-Few Saturday

- Spiritual Sunday

Mentality Monday

How often do you hear people complain about Mondays? Every Sunday night is a depressing reminder of the upcoming week. And on Monday morning, people show up to work dreading the start of another week.

Is that really how you want to live your life?

Many years ago, I learned about T.G.I.M, which stands for "Thank God It's Monday." T.G.I.M. founder Eric Thomas created the concept after seeing the huge difference in coworkers between Fridays and Mondays. [48] You can watch videos of Eric talking about why most people dread Mondays in the next course assignments section.

Mondays are the start to a new week. And each week, you have an opportunity to create something great; earn a paycheck; improve your relationships and health. And it all starts on Monday. So instead of dreading Monday, view it as an opportunity for a fresh start.

You don't need a New Year to start a resolution. Start a resolution each Monday and you'll put those weeks together to create an amazing year.

When you start Mondays with a mindset of success, it carries through to the rest of your week.

Mentality Monday Assignments

1. Watch Eric Thomas' video about T.G.I.M: https://dailylifeuniversity.wordpress.com/daily-life-university/thank-god-its-monday/. [49]

2. Check out our *Daily Life University* Facebook Group every Monday for the article or video of the week. [50]

Grati-Tuesday

Once your Monday is over, Tuesday still marks the beginning of your week. And it's important to continue Monday's momentum.

The mission of Grati-Tuesday is to look at everything with a positive attitude. Doing so will create positive thoughts which you'll inevitably demonstrate to others.

It's hard to feel stressed, sad, or mad when you're showing gratitude towards life. It's so important to feel grateful for what you have. Just being alive in America makes you more blessed than most people in the world. And adding habits like those presented in *Five Minute Journal* can help remind you of the three things you're grateful for. [41]

When it comes to gratitude, don't just be grateful for your possessions or money – because these are fleeting. Be grateful for the relationships in your life, the fact that you have a job, and the fact that you're healthy. And when you show gratitude towards others, you'll make a difference in their lives as well as your own.

It's hard to justify ditching class after you realize how blessed you are to be receiving an education. It's hard to be mad at your significant other when you're thankful you have a relationship. It's hard to be annoyed by your parents once you're thankful your parents care about you. It's hard to be negative at your job once you realize many people can't find work. It's hard to feel insecure about being out of shape when you at least show up to the gym and do something about it.

Be grateful.

Grati-Tuesday Assignments

1. Every Tuesday, read or watch something you find uplifting. Spread your cheer towards others. When someone asks you how you're doing, don't just say "okay" or "fine." Tell them you're doing amazing.

2. Smile at a stranger today. Count your blessings.

3. Check out our *Daily Life University* Facebook Group every Tuesday for the article or video of the week. [50]

Wellness Wednesday

Wednesday marks the middle of your workweek. This is a great reminder to stay on track with your goals, reflect, and recalibrate. Wednesday is also the day to improve your health. It doesn't matter how successful you are if you can't enjoy life because of poor health.

If you don't have your health, nothing else matters.

I encourage you to check out the below-listed documentaries:

1. *Forks Over Knives* – Almost every illness is preventable or curable through diet and exercise. [51]

2. *Food Inc.* – The food industry is not concerned about the health of consumers, only its bottom-line. [52]

3. *Supersize Me* – Fast food is literally killing people. [53]

4. *Hungry For Change* – The food industry's worst secrets about the Food and Drug Administration, sugar, and what consumers should be eating. [54]

5. *Fat, Sick, and Nearly Dead* – The power of juicing for a long and healthy life. [42]

In addition, I encourage you to read and bookmark these websites:

1. Food, Inc.: http://www.takepart.com/foodinc [55]

2. Prevent Disease: http://preventdisease.com/ [56]

3. Forks Over Knives: http://www.forksoverknives.com/ [57]

4. 4 Hour Body: http://fourhourbody.com/ [58]

5. The Cutco Kitchen: http://www.cutcokitchen.com/ [59]

6. Mind Body Green: http://www.mindbodygreen.com/ [60]

Your goal on Wednesdays is learn about health and wellness. Your body and energy are the most important resources you have at your disposal. It doesn't matter how talented a student or worker you are if you can't show up because you're sick. It doesn't matter how great of a husband or wife you are if you don't have the energy or health to be there for your family.

To close out this section on Wellness Wednesday, check out an article from *Daily Life University* for additional food for thought regarding health: [61]

The Dirty 30 – Is your life a HALF, a THIRD, or just a FOURTH over when you turn 30?

This blog is inspired by my 30th birthday; a.k.a. the "Dirty Thirty."

I know what you're thinking; Oh man, this guy is getting old! As I turn 30, I get the feeling there are expectations with this milestone. I should trade in my party hat, be busy with a family, work a 9-5 job, put on a few pounds, feel more tired – and, you guessed it, I should feel old.

Don't get me wrong, the aging process has started. I definitely don't feel 21 anymore. Recovering after a crazy night out with friends takes much longer than when I was in college. The aches and pains our elders tell us about, they are real. After a day of football or basketball with the guys, I struggle just bending over. I have even seen a few grey hairs pop up.

Maybe you can relate?

Despite all of these aging signs, I'm excited! I know that I'm going to live to be over 100 years old and I plan to enjoy it. Only a quarter of my life is over, and this is a time to celebrate being **30 years young**. You and I should focus not on what society expects at 30, but rather, what do the rest of our lives have in store. Recognize that your party days are over and focus on your future – these are just steps forward. Start creating an idea of new things you want to accomplish and get excited about the possibilities.

Fill your life with positivity! We will all stay younger longer and live a more fulfilled, vibrant life if we focus our minds. Choose to live a healthy life by nourishing your body with healthy food and regular exercise. It's important to know that we choose to be young. "Our bodies are a reflection of our lifestyle and mentality."

We are all meant to live long lives. Unfortunately, American culture is robbing years of life from some individuals through unhealthy lifestyle choices. Back in Biblical times, it was common for people to surpass 100 years of age. This was all done without the modern medicine and healthcare that we rely on today. You would think our society would be living longer with how many resources we have access to today.

Wellness Wednesday Assignments

1. Go to *Daily Life University* Wellness Wednesday page and watch the videos from Hal Elrod and Tony Robbins: https://dailylifeuniversity.wordpress.com/daily-life-university/wellness-wednesday/. [62]

2. Check out our *Daily Life University* Facebook Group every Wednesday for the article or video of the week. [50]

Thriving Relationships Thursday

Your relationships are one of the most important areas of your life. This includes your friends, family, and significant other.

The quality of your life is determined by the quality of your relationships.

All of us could use some help getting better at connecting with people, whether it's building rapport, using active listening, or being engaged in the conversation. This is what every Thursday is all about: improving your relationship skills.

Here are some tools and resources to help you understand people and what it takes to foster great relationships.

Emotional Intelligence (EQ)

According to Hal Elrod: "*Research has proven conclusively that what distinguishes the happiest, healthiest, and most successful individuals is not IQ, skills, or talent. Rather it is Emotional Intelligence (also known as "EQ"), and it is as much as three times more important than IQ and technical skills – combined!*"[63]

An individual with high Emotional Intelligence (EQ) can effectively recognize and control his or her emotions, and has an intuitive feel for the feelings of others, too. It is very advantageous to refine your EQ skills not only for the relationships in your life, but for overall success.

Read some tips about how to grow and develop your EQ skills in this article from *Psychology Today:* [64]

https://www.psychologytoday.com/blog/communication-success/201410/how-increase-your-emotional-intelligence-6-essentials

Next, let's talk about thriving in intimate relationships.

Would you believe most people spend more time planning for their wedding and honeymoon than they do their marriage? This is why the next book I'm writing – with the help of my wife – is going to be based on doing relationships right after doing them all wrong in college.

For those looking to take their marriage or relationship to the next level, consider reading *The Five Love Languages*. [65] This book provides an insightful quiz and easy-to-apply concepts for you and your partner to understand each other's needs, improve your communication, and improve your relationship.

All of us have probably heard the expression that the quality of our lives is determined by the quality of our relationships. It's totally true. And we need to foster these relationships by making sure we're making time to understand the people in our lives, giving them the attention they deserve, and not being afraid to show them affection.

At the end of the day, this is what being human is all about.

Thriving Relationships Thursday Assignments

1. Use Thursdays to spend time with a family member, call and catch up with a friend, or set a date night with your significant other.

2. Pick one of the ideas above (EQ or Five Love Languages) and begin investing time in learning about it every Thursday.

3. Check out our *Daily Life University* Facebook Group every Thursday for the article or video of the week. [50]

Financial Abundance Friday

Chances are, you get paid on Fridays. But the truth is, you either control your money or you let money control you. And Fridays are the perfect day to learn how to control your money and build wealth. Yes, this does mean saving your money and not spending it all over the weekend.

There are many great books and blogs out there on money management and financial success. One of the best programs I have experienced on general money management is Dave Ramsey's *Financial Peace University.* [66]

And for college students, Rachel Cruze – Dave Ramsey's daughter – has developed programs aimed at managing money as a young adult. If you're in high school or college, you can find great resources on Rachel's website at www.rachelcruze.com. [67]

When it comes to building wealth once you have money, Robert Kiyosaki has many amazing books including classics like *Rich Dad, Poor Dad* and *Cash Flow Quadrant.*

Here is an excerpt from an article from ***Daily Life University*** that gives you a taste of what you'll learn on Financial Abundance Fridays: [68]

How to Cover Your Expenses and Stay Out of Debt

With rising tuition costs, college students are graduating with more debt than ever before. Not only are young people struggling to pay back their student loans after graduation, but they are also struggling during college as they rack up credit card debt because of their limited experience budgeting the little money they have.

So, who's to blame? No one and everyone at the same time! Unfortunately, being in debt and living outside of your means is common in today's

Western culture. Often, you learn poor money management skills from your family and friends.

So, can you break the cycle? Of course! Through my personal experiences taking Dave Ramsey's *Financial Peace University* course, [66] learning from Tony Robbins, and working with college students for the last 13+ years while also being a college graduate myself, I can tell you it is certainly possible. Here are four steps to begin covering *all* of your expenses *and* start saving:

STEP 1 – Write Down and Categorize All Your Monthly Expenses

If you have no idea how much you spend, look at your bank statements for the last month or two to get a feel for where your money is going. Then, print your monthly statements and assign a category to each expense, such as food, entertainment, and bills to track where you're spending money.

STEP 2 – Download the Mint.com App [69]

This app is a great tool to link your spending together. I believe this is one the best free tools for basic budgeting.

The Mint app allows you to get a snapshot of your debts, expenses, and bank accounts. You'll be reminded of upcoming bills and low balances of an account, and you can set up a budget for each category to make sure you stay on track.

A lot of people overspend because they aren't aware of their spending or cash flow. The ability to open the app and see what you just spent that day or if you're on track with your budget is half the battle. With the Mint app, you will actually be aware of your spending and, as a result, be able to better manage your money.

STEP 3 – Get Creative to Earn Extra Money!

Once you start noticing your spending patterns, you may realize you need to find a flexible job that will allow you to make more money. However, you probably have a hectic and busy schedule already and don't want to work a minimum wage job just to make ends meet.

But if you discovered in Step 1 and Step 2 that your spending exceeds your income, it's time to make a change.

Ideas to make extra money:

1. Donate plasma

2. Sell items on Craigslist or eBay

3. Freelance by doing things you're good at, such as cleaning, driving, or writing.

4. Join a FREE direct sales company like Cutco. Many reps work just 10 -15 hours a week and take home $1,000+ a month.

Don't let the excuses such as, "I don't know what to do," or, "I don't have time," keep you from staying out of debt. Yes, everyone is busy. But have you ever noticed how it's possible to make time for what is important? It's time to make your finances as important as anything else in your life.

STEP 4 – Stick to a Budget and Start Saving

Dave Ramsey lays it out well with his "Ben vs. Arthur" example. The chart below shows how early investing into a retirement fund can have a huge impact on the amount of money you'll accumulate over your lifetime. Even though Ben invests only $16,000 less than Arthur's $76,000, Ben ended up with an *extra $750,000* in retirement, with because he started saving earlier.

With your new budget, extra income sources, and savings goals, begin investing in a Roth IRA retirement fund with whatever money you have available. The most important thing is to start – and the best time to start is *right now!*

The result of starting a retirement fund at 19 vs. 26 is over $750,000 at age 65.

Financial Abundance Friday Assignments

1. Download the Mint.com app. [69]

2. Start listening to material from Dave Ramsey, Robert Kiyosaki, or other finance resources of your choice.

3. Check out our *Daily Life University* Facebook Group every Friday for the article or video of the week. [50]

Select Few Saturday

Select Few Saturday is exactly what you think: It's for the select few who choose to **chase their dreams and improve over the weekend,** while most party away their weekend.

The opportunity of Saturday is to really get ahead of the majority. Most young people spend their Saturdays sleeping in or recovering from a hangover. What if you got ahead by investing in yourself? What if Saturday morning was your morning to get your most important tasks done? Whether it's mastering a new skill, completing homework, or doing the laundry and grocery shopping, use your Saturday wisely.

Most people wish they were successful but few wake up and *do* something about it.

I was a part of this way of life in college because it's just what everybody did. It was so easy to stay up until 3:00 in the morning partying on a Friday night. Then, I woke up a hungover mess at noon on Saturday. After watching football all day, I'd go out and party again on Saturday night.

But this way of life does not get you anywhere. It will cost you a lot of money, produce regrets, and hurt your health. This is why being passionate about having a productive Saturday morning sets you apart from the pack.

Today, I start most of my Saturday mornings with hot yoga. Getting in the right state of mind with a great workout first thing on Saturday sets me up for a productive morning and afternoon.

If you don't want to be like most people, don't do what most people do.

Many people view their Friday and Saturday nights with a very short-term outlook. I learned this many years ago from Matthew Kelly's *The Rhythm of Life*, a powerful book about choosing long-term happiness over short-term pleasure. [70]

Partying may be fun in the moment, but you usually don't feel good about it once the party is over. Eating a chocolate cake might taste really good in the moment, but as soon as you're done eating it, it's not going to continue making you happy. And if you're a chronic snooze button pusher, it may feel amazing to do it in the moment. But when you're rushing to get to work or class, your whole day is thrown off. None of these habits help your happiness or long-term success.

On the other hand, if you resist that chocolate cake and reach for an apple, you feel great, because you've shifted to a healthy way of living. You may want to stay on the couch instead of working out, but once you're exercising, you feel great.

"Wow, I really regret that workout" – said nobody, ever.

It may not feel good in the moment to choose to stay in on a Saturday night and get ahead on your project, but it can transform your productivity. When you finish that project and eliminate the weekend stress, your whole week will be different. You'll have traded one day of momentary happiness for seven days of contentment and freedom.

Choosing to make daily choices for long-term happiness rather than short-term pleasure will transform your way of life.

Select Few Saturday Assignments

1. What do you never have time to do? Do it this Saturday morning.

2. Check out Peter Voogd's website, where I first learned about the Select Few Saturdays concept: https://peterjvoogd.com/about/. [71]

3. Check out our *Daily Life University* Facebook Group every Saturday for the article or video of the week. [50]

Spiritual Sunday

Sunday is your day of rest. Whether or not you are religious, it's important to rest and recover at least one day a week. One of the most important aspects of life is to feel at peace and keep a higher purpose in mind. People with inner peace enjoy life more and are much happier.

For those of you who are religious, I found the YouVersion Bible app to be very helpful to my daily devotions. [72] It really helps me get my daily fill of God. I also attend an amazing church that always helps me feel refreshed and loved. But whether it's God or something else, life has more meaning when you believe in a greater cause.

Since I was raised in a Christian home, I think of church and God when I plan my Sundays. If you're not religious, it's still important to have a sense of purpose in life, to help you find inner peace and hope for your future.

Today, it's easy to become negative. Whether you believe in negative universal forces, the devil, or anything else, it's important to fill yourself with positive energy. I'm at a point in my life where if I don't attend church, I don't feel fulfilled. So, I treat Sunday as a reset day. It's the day when I fill up my energy cup, remind myself of my higher purpose, and plan the upcoming week.

What is important is your purpose in this world. Consider this on Sundays, and allow yourself to go into the next week with the right intentions.

Spiritual leaders I love learning from include Andy Stanley of North Point Ministries, Steven Furtick of Elevation Church, Shawn Hennessy of Life Church Green Bay, and Francis Chan of Eternity Bible College.

God, grant me the serenity to accept the things I cannot change; courage to change the things I can; and wisdom to know the difference.

Spiritual Sunday Assignments

1. Start attending a local church or community group that aligns with your higher purpose and meaning.

2. Check out our **Daily Life University** Facebook Group every Sunday for the article or video of the week. [50]

Daily Life University Conclusion

The *Daily Life University* program is life changing. Your mind is probably overloaded with information right now and you may be asking yourself how you could possibly implement this system into your life. I know; it's a lot to take in at once.

In the next course, you'll get some crucial tips on how to become more productive and learn to systemize your success on a daily basis.

**Remember, being successful and growing
doesn't happen by accident.**

Note: If you're not enrolled in college and at least 18 years old, you can skip to course 12. This next section covers an opportunity open to students.

The Daily Life University Scholarship

With this program having "University" in its title, it only makes sense that there's a scholarship to accompany it.

After launching the *Daily Life University* website in 2014, I thought of a really cool way to give back to those who read my daily advice: Offering a scholarship for students just like you.

To help you with your education and future successes, *Daily Life University* offers a scholarship for students to help out with today's increasing college tuition costs. The scholarship is easy to apply for, especially considering how far you've gotten in this book.

I believe this is the most impactful scholarship you can earn, because it encourages students to make lasting changes in their lives. This scholarship encourages students to think about life as a daily choice that either adds or eliminates habits to drastically improve their life. Even if a student isn't awarded the scholarship but applies the principles of *Daily Life University*, they've won.

Every semester, *Daily Life University* awards one $250 scholarship to a college student who wants to improve his or her life.

Fill out the short application and write a one-page essay answering the following questions:

1. *Daily Life Habit:* What is one habit that, if added daily, would drastically improve your life and why?

2. Post a picture to Instagram/Twitter/Facebook of you doing your daily habit and tag http://www.DailyLifeUniversity.com or #DailyLifeU

My hope is the scholarship allows thousands of young people to receive their own *"improved life scholarship."* During the application process, you will have to dig deep and think about what can help you live your daily life better. And *Daily Life University* exists to help people grow into the best version of themselves.

So, at the end of each semester (December 1st & May 1st), *Daily Life*

University will pick one winner for its scholarship with the hope the $250 will help the student start the *Daily Life Habit* he or she wrote about, and provide a few extra bucks to use towards personal growth.

Scholarship Qualifications:

1. Must be 18 years old.

2. Must be enrolled in a college.

3. Must submit the online application and one-page essay here.

4. Can submit a new application every semester.

5. Add yourself to the *Daily Life University* group on Facebook and follow #DailyLifeU.

6. Take a picture of you performing your daily habit, post it to at least one social media platform, and tag www.DailyLifeUniversity.com or #DailyLifeU.

Process:

1. Your application and essay will be reviewed by multiple judges at the end of the semester.

2. The winner will be announced via email and social media to all the applicants on either December 1st or May 1st.

3. The check will be mailed to the scholarship winner.

4. You may submit a new application each semester.

5. In the meantime, continue following the *Daily Life University* blog and join our Facebook group to receive life-changing information.

Molly receives her *Daily Life University* scholarship award. Congratulations, Molly!

Shown above is Molly Kaprelian of UW-Oshkosh, the first recipient of the *Daily Life University* scholarship, December 2014.

Now that you know about the scholarship, pass it along to someone else who can benefit from it.

Daily Life University Scholarship Assignments

1. Apply for DLU Scholarship if you are in college at www.DailyLifeUniversityScholarship.com.

2. Share this scholarship opportunity with at least one person.

COURSE 12

How to Gain More Hours Each Day

Do you ever feel like there are not enough hours in the day?

You may think, "If only I had one more hour, then I could get everything done." Good news! There actually are enough hours in a day. This lesson will show you how to find them.

All of us have the same amount of time as Bill Gates, Oprah Winfrey, and the President of the United States. There are many people who are even busier than us but get more accomplished. Here's the secret: it's not about the amount of time we have, but rather how we use the time that is important.

Back in my college days, I believed I was an expert at juggling priorities. If friends asked me to hangout, I would say no problem. After all, homework could wait, right? But I found myself forgetting to do things and feeling guilty when I hadn't started on homework assignments. It was hard to stay true to my word because I had no schedule or deadline. What I needed was a lesson in time management.

About 10 years ago, I began focusing on improving my time management skills. To maintain my daily schedule, I kept a planner to track all my homework, appointments, upcoming events, and reminders. This method, though effective, was time-consuming and redundant. I grew tired of rewriting my recurring activities, so I started using Google Calendar.

Here is a very productive and busy example from Alex Filkouski, a freshman at UW-Oshkosh. He was the #6 Cutco All-American Scholarship winner, selected out of over 50,000 applicants.

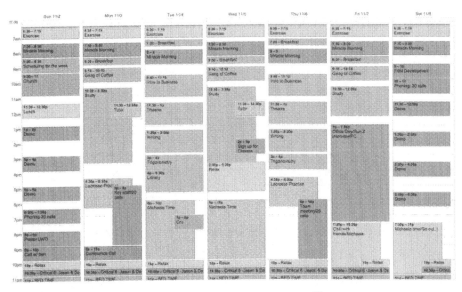

Alex's schedule on Google Calendar. [73]

All of us have 168 hours in a week.
It's how we use those hours that matters.

Using a typical college student as an example, let's break down a great application of hours per week:

- **49 hours:** Sleeping seven hours each night.

- **7 hours:** Performing the Miracle Morning one hour per day.

- **3.5 hours:** Exercising 30 minutes per day.

- **14 hours:** Eating meals and snacks for a total of 2 hours each day; don't forget about breakfast!

- **10 hours:** Getting ready for one hour in the morning and 30 minutes at night, assuming you don't just roll out of bed 10 minutes before classes start.

- **5 hours:** Participating in church, clubs, and other extracurricular groups.

- **45 hours:** 18 credit-hours worth of classes and homework if you're a student or a full time job with commute

- **12 hours:** Spending time with your significant other or friends a few times each week.

- **7 hours:** Playing video games and watching TV one hour a day.

- **All Day, Every Day:** Social media scrolling while simultaneously doing many of the things above.

This schedule adds up to just 152 of the 168 hours of the week, meaning 16 hours remain. Most of these estimates are conservative and don't necessarily represent the average student's or young professional's schedule. Consider, for example, the student that only has 12 credit hours, doesn't perform his Miracle Morning, and doesn't have a significant other. That's an extra 23 hours available each week. Consider, also, that many of the tasks above can be combined. An example of a combined task is someone who spends time with his or her significant other while having lunch or watching TV. Based on the schedule above, that person has an extra 15 hours every week to fill.

With that said, I'd like to leave you with a quote from Marc Levy:

Imagine there is a bank, which credits your account each morning with $86,400. It doesn't carry over a balance from day to day, it doesn't allow you to keep cash, and, every evening, deletes whatever part of the amount you didn't use during those 24 hours. What would you do?

You would, of course, take out every last penny, every day.

Well, all of us have such a bank. Its name is TIME and every morning, it credits you with 86,400 seconds. Every night it writes off, as a loss, whatever amount you failed to invest. It carries over no balance. It allows no overdraft.

But each day, it opens a new account for you. If you fail to use the day's deposits, the loss is yours. There is no going back. There is no drawing against "tomorrow." You must live in the present on today's deposits.

Invest your time so you can invest the most in your health, happiness, and success. And the clock is running. [74]

Make the most of today.

You learned in this course that you can get a lot accomplished in life if you have a well-organized program. If you create a structured schedule to keep you on track, you'll make progress every day.

In the second-to-last course of the book, you'll learn about an amazing opportunity that helped me learn almost everything in this book. This next course may not be for everybody, but for those who take advantage of it at a young age, it can change their future forever, just like it did mine.

Course 12 Assignments

1. Describe what your ideal week looks like.

2. Create your ideal schedule using a calendar app or Google Calendar.

3. Keep track in your phone what you do with each hour this week. You'll be surprised how you are really using your time.

COURSE 13

The Letter That Changed My Life

In this course, you'll learn where I developed the success mentality I credit with my success. Today, it is one of the biggest influences in my life.

Note: If you are past your college days and don't really care about my past, you can jump to the commencement course 14.

If you read this far in the book, you obviously care about your future. You think differently than most young people. You understand that you need to personally grow to get ahead in life. You understand that college and your job are very important influences to the individual you are becoming.

Remember, you are the common denominator in each area of your life.

In every situation, every class, in every job, you are with yourself at all times. Therefore, it's important that you are "the best version of yourself," as put brilliantly by Matthew Kelly. [75]

With that said, I want to share with you a recommendation that helped me transform into the best version of myself.

Up to this point in your life, have you had a hard time finding a job that's flexible enough for your busy life and school schedule? Have you been paid what you're worth? Are you sick of putting in extra effort compared to your coworkers and not being rewarded for it?

I did. And I found a solution which I'd like to share with you.

Back in 2004, I started working for Cutco. Besides my faith and my family, this job is the most far-reaching influential choice in my life. Cutco has challenged me to become a better person. I learned to overcome adversity and believe in myself. I learned to communicate better with people and to be more confident. I learned to manage my schedule and to be more productive with my time. I learned how to set goals and how to accomplish them. I learned how to make work fun. Basically, I learned everything you just read about in this book.

In 2004, after my freshman year in college, I got a letter in the mail while working with my father as an electrician. I love my dad – but I hated manual labor. I had no idea what this random company did but I thought, "why not apply and see what happens?" That was one of the best decisions of my life.

On June 12, 2004, I began working at Cutco. I had no idea what I was doing but I came in with a great work ethic and a positive attitude. Yes, my parents questioned my decision to sell knives. "Friends" teased me because it was a different kind of job that they didn't understand yet. Most of my friends were flipping burgers, folding clothes, or mowing lawns that summer. They didn't understand the concept of sales, business, or high-end kitchen products.

When I started the job, I was really nervous and unsure of how well I'd do. I told myself to give it two weeks and, if I wasn't doing well or enjoying the job, I'd go find another job like most of my friends had. I am so glad I gave it a shot.

After making mistakes but building confidence, I ended up making $6,000 in two months and was the number #4 sales representative in my office.

After that summer, I went back to school for football and track so I wasn't able to work until winter break. Over winter break, my manager asked me if I wanted to be an assistant manager. I was excited and, of course, I said yes!

That summer I became a selling assistant manager. I absolutely loved it. I was in the office a few days a week coaching reps. Then, I was out selling a few days of the week and leading by example. I was excited to do really well. However, I felt far more rewarded to see someone who I'd helped influence have that success. That summer, I worked really hard and earned $23,000 as a 20-year-old college student.

I decided to retire from sports. I wasn't on a path to playing professionally had gotten injured a few times. Since I wasn't on scholarship with a Division III team, I chose to use my free time to work and make money.

I continued to work around my school schedule that next year. Then, I accepted the opportunity to run a branch office in La Crosse, WI. It was an amazing opportunity to negotiate for an office space, hire a receptionist staff, interview interview hundreds of people, and train dozens for the job.

That was one of the toughest summers – also being one of the most rewarding – of my life. That summer, I learned what it meant to be an entrepreneur. I learned what it took to run a business. I learned how to invest in people, manage them, and help them succeed. Even though I made a ton of mistakes, I grew tremendously as a person.

At this point, my resume was stacked. I was about to graduate with a sports management degree and I had many opportunities for work. I had switched my major six times and wasn't sure exactly what I wanted to do. So, in 2008, when I graduated, I decided to open a Cutco district office.

I've been running the office now for 10+ years and absolutely love it. I feel so blessed about my position. The most rewarding aspect is the impact I have on young people. Given the current culture of most colleges and universities, I firmly believe that our nation needs to come together and help develop its young people.

Without Cutco, I wouldn't have learned how to manage my time or connect with people. Without Cutco, I wouldn't have realized the importance of personal growth. Without Cutco, I wouldn't have traveled around the world.

At this point, I have been on 25+ international company trips. I have attended over 50 personal growth conferences with and without Vector Marketing, which is the company that distributes Cutco products. I have read over 100 books that have changed the trajectory of my life. And I've met so many amazing people. Whether someone sticks with Cutco for a few weeks, a few months during the summer, or a few years after graduating, they will learn so much. And who knows, it may even become a career for them like it has for me.

There are so many amazing people who do great things in their careers or businesses after being with Cutco. The list is long and it includes Olympians and professional athletes, actors like Michael C. Hall, comedians like Daniel Tosh, best-selling authors like Hal Elrod, motivational speakers like Peter Voogd, world-class sales trainers like Jon Berghoff, the founders of companies such as Uber, charities like the Front Row Foundation started by Jon Vroman, and countless other successful business owners.

You can find more information about this great opportunity at www.GetSkillsForLife.com.

In this course, you learned about the experience that took my life to the next level. In the final course, you will be celebrating. It will be like graduation day – except this time, you'll be graduating to a new level of life.

Course 13 Assignments

1. If you are looking for work or have a friend who is hard-working and positive, apply at www.WorkForStudents.com for the nearest location. Vector offices are located across the United States and Canada.

COURSE 14

Commencement:
This is Just the Beginning of Your New Life

Well, it's time.

It's time for your graduation. The wonderful part is that this graduation is not after four years and tens of thousands of dollars, though it may be worth that and more. There are no awkward family photos and no odd-looking caps and gowns. This is about you. After reading this book, it's time to start making positive changes.

You may be thinking, where are the "Success Secrets to Thrive in my 20's and 30's?" As you read through this book, you learned a ton of ways to grow as an individual.

One of the greatest success secrets in life is continual progress on yourself by investing time in personal growth.

If you implement all these concepts into your daily life, you'll become a super successful person. If you do Miracle Morning, stick to a structured daily schedule, and grow through the *Daily Life University* program, I promise you will be a better person, parent, significant other, and worker!

Now that you've graduated from *Daily Life University*, it's time to figure out what you want your life to look like. It's time to figure out what you want to do moving forward from this moment, and to make sure this is not just another cool book you read and do nothing with.

Looking ahead to the rest of your life, it's imperative to have a vision. The Bible says, "Where there is no vision, the people perish" (Proverbs 29:18). [76] Most of us don't get what we want simply because we don't know what we want. We've never written down a list of life goals.

In his book, *The Circle Maker,* Mark Batterson explains how crucial setting goals is for our future success. He says, *"We've never defined success for ourselves. And our dreams are as nebulous as cumulus clouds... The brain is a goal-seeking organism. Setting a goal creates structural tension in your brain, which will seek to close the gap between where you are and where you want to be, who you are and who you want to become. If you don't set goals, your mind will become stagnant. Goal-setting is a good stewardship of you right brain imagination."* Creating goals helps us to achieve what we seek, whereas a lack setting goals allows our minds to dwindle away. [77]

When setting goals, keep them measurable. Goals are a practical way of dreaming big. For example, getting in shape is not a goal; it's a dream. Running a half marathon, however, is a measurable goal because you know you've accomplished it when you cross the finish line (and you'll get in shape along the way if you train for it).

"Goals are dreams with deadlines. And these deadlines, especially if your personality is anything like mine, are really lifelines. Without a deadline, I would never accomplish anything because I'd be just dreaming of other dreams without taking action. And that's why so many dreams go unaccomplished. If you don't give your dreams a deadline, it will be dead

before you know it. Deadlines keep dreams alive. Deadlines bring dreams back to life." [77]

Keys to Figure out your Life Goals

Look to Others

It's hard to pull life goals out of thin air, so I recommend looking at the life goals of others. Don't cut and paste someone else's goals, but looking to the goals of others is an efficient way to generate your own ideas.

Think in Categories

I almost always begin writing down my goals by breaking them down into categories. Categories such as adventure, work, health, education, family, faith, legacy, travel, and financial help to organize your thinking and get you started.

Be Specific

If a goal isn't measurable, you will not have a way of knowing whether or not you've accomplished it. Losing weight isn't a goal if you don't have a target weight within a target timeline. One of the ways I've increased the specificity of my goals is by attaching ages to some of them (for example, I want to go skydiving by age 35 and have two rental properties by age 40).

It may be difficult or daunting to attach specific ages to some of your life goals; however, I encourage you to try it. It's better to aim high and fall short than aim low and hit the target. And it's completely fine to make revisions. J. C. Penny was quoted as saying, *"Give me a stock clerk with a goal, and I will give you a man who will make history. Give me a man without a goal, and I will give you a stock clerk."* [78]

Write them Down

Something powerful happens when you verbalize goal, whether in a conversation or on paper. On more than one occasion, I've been able to achieve a goal almost immediately after setting it because I was aware of it and focused on it. When you write down a goal, it holds you accountable.

Also, at some point in the process of goal-setting, you need to muster the courage to verbalize it. I've found that verbalizing my dreams and talking about them with others often speeds up the process and helps me to achieve that goal.

Think Long-Term

Most of us overestimate what we can accomplish in a year, but we underestimate what we can accomplish in ten years. If we want to dream big, we need to think long. If you want to dream until the day you die, you need to set goals that take a lifetime to achieve. And it's never too late to start.

The sad truth is that most people spend more time planning their summer vacation than they do planning the rest of their life.

Instead of letting things happen, goals help us make things happen. Instead of living by default, goals help us live by design. Instead of living out of memory, goals help us live out of imagination.

Life Goals List

So now it's time to make your own life goals list. Get out a piece of paper or open a word document and get started. I'm going to ask that you just stay open-minded and write down anything that comes to your mind that you want for your life. It doesn't have to be perfect. This is just a rough draft. I am constantly modifying my life goals list.

I also add the random, cool things I've done as I accomplished them. As a result, almost half of my list was added after I had already accomplished the

CONQUER THE POST-COLLEGE PASSION SLUMP

goals. I have done a ton of cool things that I didn't originally think I'd do. Keeping this list helps remind myself to be grateful for the many great things I've done in life. I am able to feel good about my life every time I look at my life goals list.

Now I'm sure you don't care about my dreams and goals in life, but I've included my life goals list below to help get you started. I list out my dreams, and as I accomplish them, I italicize them. This helps me to visually see what I have and have not yet accomplished. Then, from my list, I like to focus on which goals I would like to accomplish in the year ahead. I then move those specific goals to the top of my page under a "This Year" heading, which helps me narrow my focus. This way I don't get distracted by the hundreds of goal I want to accomplish.

My Dreams and Goals for this Year and Life

Dreams for 2018

1. Master 12 books every year (Circle Maker, One Minute Manager, The One Thing, Total Money Makeover, Cash Flow Quadrant, Crucial Conversations, Making Marriage Work, etc...)

2. Follow Tony Robbins health plan and exercise every day (Maintain under 185 lbs with a 6 pack)

3. Save $50,000+

4. 5+ big trips a year

   a. Las Vegas P.Banquet, SLC-Hollywood, Switzerland, Germany, Punta Cana

5. Publish my first book (this one)

6. Buy my first duplex

7. Start 2nd book – *Finding the One* – How to Do it Right After Learning it All Wrong (relationship book with Abby)

8. $1.25 Million+ Office and $700,000 New Business and $1.7 Million District

9. Miracle Morning Daily (5:00-7:00 a.m.)

10. Give back $25,000 (11%) to charities and tithe

Adventure

1. *Fly in a helicopter*
2. *Electric run*
3. *Attend a Tony Robbins Event*
4. *See the David in Florence Italy*
5. *See Pompeii*
6. *See the Colosseum, Vatican, Spanish steps and others*
7. Sign up for Master University/Date with Destiny (2018)
8. *National world record Zumba Class at Lambeau*
9. *Line Dance in Nashville, TN at the famous Wild Horse Saloon*
10. *Go to a Vanderbilt homecoming football game*
11. Guinness World Record
12. Front Row Foundation Event
13. *Polar plunge*
14. *Donate 40 meals to impoverished families*
15. Skydiving with Josh Curry
16. *Indoor skydiving*
17. *Speak at Miller Park*
18. *Swim with sharks and stingrays*
19. *Swim in the ocean at midnight under the stars*
20. *Get a standing ovation*
21. *Get on the field and big screen at the new Dallas Cowboy stadium*

22. Learn how to salsa and ballroom dance

23. Hot air balloon ride

24. Go canyoning in Switzerland or Iceland

25. Train ride through the Swiss Alps

26. *Kid Cudi and Kanye West concert*

27. *Whitewater rafting in CO*

28. *Timeflies Tuesday concert*

29. Get a patent

30. Be on the floor of a basketball game

31. *Parasail*

32. *Bungee jump*

33. *Scuba diving*

34. *Washington D.C.*

35. *St. Louis Arch*

36. Hang Glide

37. Snowboard at the top five places in the U.S.

38. Go to the Super Bowl

39. Go to a Final Four basketball game

40. Attend an All-Star basketball game

41. Attend the Grammys

42. Attend the Oscars

43. Be at the opening of a new movie

44. Attend an Olympic Games

45. Learn guitar and piano

46. Learn Spanish

47. *Ride in a stretch hummer limo*

48. Live to be over 100

49. Have my funeral be a celebration

50. *Tour the Guinness factory*

51. *Tour the Cliffs of Moher and Ashford Castle*

52. *See Hollywood*

53. Attend an X Games

54. Drive a Bugatti

55. *Attend the Big Give in Chicago*

56. *Get paid for giving first speech*

57. *Jump off the cliffs at Rick's Café in Jamaica*

58. *Bike across the Golden Gate Bridge in San Francisco*

59. *Attend a Warriors game when they come back from 27 points down*

60. Have lunch with Will Smith, Kobe Bryant, Justin TimberlakeTony Robbins, and Matthew West

61. Backpack in Europe for a couple months with spouse

62. Houseboat cruise down the Mississippi with friends

63. *Have my 30th bday party celebrating my life only being 25% over*

64. *Give a speech at a statewide WASC event*

65. *Kress Nightclub in L.A.*

66. Pasadena for Rose Bowl

67. See mount Rushmore

College/School

1. *Graduate from college with higher than a 3.0 GPA*

2. *Play college football and run track and field*

3. *All-Conference Athlete*

4. *Make it to State*

5. *Be on the cover of a newspaper*

6. *Be on the news*

7. *Best Athlete at Waukesha North award*

Cutco/Work

1. *Win All-American Scholarship*

2. *Sir Lancelott Winner*

3. *Run a Branch*

4. *Train an FSM/BM/DM*

5. *President's Banquet*

6. *Have a $1 million year and win a Rolex*

7. Have a million dollar summer

8. *Train an All American*

9. *Start an annual healthy Cutco cooking clinic*

10. *$250,000 in career sales by 30*

11. *Hit Court of Honor*

12. *DM Advisory Board Member*

13. *Hit Hall of Fame by 32*

14. Triple crown service award

15. Division Manager by age 35

Financial

1. *Save $20,000+ a year*

2. *Earn a $150,000 1099*

3. *Earn $200,000 on 1099 in 2017*

4. Earn $250,000 1099 in 2018

5. Get to over $4 million saved and live off my interest by age 57

a. $1 million saved by age 40 and save $50,000 a year

b. $500,000 saved by age 35 and save $30,000 a year

6. Buy my first property by age 33

Life/Family

1. *Get married to the woman of my dreams*

2. *Wait to have sex with her until marriage*

3. Cooked meals four times a week

4. Hot tub, fireplace, sauna

5. Live on a lake or a hill or ocean

6. Self driving/green car

7. Saltwater fish tank

8. Smart home

9. *Date night every week*

10. Be the greatest influence in my family's life

11. Have a peaceful cabin

Spiritual

1. *Quiet time every day (finish 25+ YouVersion devotionals a year)*

2. *Church every Sunday and observe the Sabbath*

3. *Lead a Christian workshop/group*

4. *Positive uplifting K-Love music every day*

5. *Meditate every day*

6. *Tithe 10% back to the church*

7. Pray Bold Prayers Daily
8. Serve and become less selfish

Physical

1. *Weigh a solid 185 lbs*
2. *Less than 15% body fat*
3. *Eat healthy (less processed food, more fruits and veggies, like Tony Robbins' health plan)*
4. *Fast food no more than two times per week*
5. *Work out at least six days a week, forever*
6. Compete in a triathlon, half marathon, or Tough Mudder
7. Six pack
8. *Be able to do a flip*
9. *Have a 36-inch vertical*
10. *Don't buy meat or dairy*
11. *Complete p90x*
12. *Be able to do back flips*
13. *Complete a 5K*

Becoming a Better Person/Legacy

1. *Read/listen to one book a month*
2. *Donate 11%+ back to church and charities*
3. Eventually live on 10% of my income and give the rest
4. *Adopt a Family for Christmas*
5. *Win the Young Professionals Future 15 award*
6. *Speak in high schools and colleges*
7. #1 winner of the Future 15 award
8. Complete ToastMasters first two books
9. *Raise $10,000 a year for charities – Front Row, Polar plunge, Lifest*

10. Technology free time 8:00 p.m. – 8:00 a.m.

11. *Three outcomes every day*

12. *Journal everyday*

13. *Write a book*

14. *Write a blog used by businesses*

15. Featured on Forbes or Business Insider

16. Have my book in Barnes and Noble

17. Get paid to speak at least 10 times a year

18. Sell over 1 million copies of books

19. Grow **Daily Life University** Facebook group to over 100,000 and have a famous person be in charge of each day

20. *Start CEO of the 920 (Christian Entrepreneurs Outfit)*

Character/Psychological/Emotional Dreams

1. More courage

2. Always positive

3. Never let fear dictate my actions

4. Integrity

5. More caring

6. Inspect what I expect

7. Never hit snooze anymore-pop right out of bed

8. Be in the moment

9. Overcome my fear of speaking

10. Be certain in myself

11. I am the average of the 5 people I surround myself with

12. I'd like to be described as charismatic, caring, passionate, smart, funny, lovable, servant leader

Travel

1. Australia
2. See the 7 wonders of the world
3. *Rome, Italy*
4. *Florence, Italy*
5. *Naples, Italy*
6. Sicily, Italy
7. *Punta Cana*
8. *Puerto Vallarta*
9. *Las Vegas*
10. Spain
11. *Amsterdam*
12. Istanbul, Turkey
13. *Budapest, Hungary*
14. *Vienna, Austria*
15. Caribbean Islands Cruise
16. *Cancun*
17. *Aruba*
18. *Riviera Maya*
19. *Cabo*
20. *Jamaica*
21. Bora Bora
22. *Prague*
23. *Costa Rica*
24. *Ireland*
25. *Hawaii*

26. See Niagara Falls

27. Egypt

28. Brazil

29. Panama – 2014

30. China

31. Japan

32. Africa

33. Galapagos Islands

34. Fiji - Tony Robbins Event with Abby

35. Iceland

36. Switzerland

37. Munich, Germany – 2018

So now, take 30 minutes to brainstorm your life goals list! If you can't do it immediately, schedule a one hour time block to do it soon. If you're married, it's empowering to do it with your spouse as well. Get out your journal and do it now!

After you spend 30 minutes brainstorming your list, spend another 30 minutes picking out the top goals you want to accomplish this year. Also, put dates on some of your goals. Maybe it's not realistic to buy your first rental property this year, but in three years it could be possible.

Print your goals and put them somewhere you can look them daily. As busy humans, we need to be reminded often of what we want. It's very easy to get distracted or choose momentary pleasures instead of choosing success.

Congratulations on finishing this book!

Most people are not disciplined or motivated enough to finish books or school. Only 42 percent of incoming freshman actually finish college. In order to put yourself in a position to really thrive in your 20's and 30's, don't stop here. To help you continue the momentum, here are some challenges:

Challenge #1: Create Your 30-Day Habit Challenge

- Identify a habit that you want to create along with your "why" for pursuing that habit. Be ready for the three phases:

  1. Unbearable (Day 1-10)

  2. Uncomfortable (Day 11-20)

  3. Unstoppable (Day 21-30)

- Track your habit every day during the 30-Day Challenge.

What are your **three new habits** you want to implement from this book?

1. _____

2. _____

3. _____

When will you start them? _____

Who will you become in 30 days when these habits become part of you?

_____

_____

_____

_____

Challenge #2: Create Your Accountability Plan

- Choose which accountability types (below) you are going to put into practice.

- Set up your system.

- Stay consistent with your system and your commitments.

- Work to intentionally build the skill of accountability.

There are five main types of accountability:

1. *You* – Holding yourself accountable

2. *Peer Accountability* – Finding a partner to hold you accountable

3. *Peer Accountability 2.0* – Leading an accountability group of peers

4. *Private Coaching* – Hiring a coach to help you set and stick to your commitments*

5. *Public Declarations* – Announcing your commitment broadly, such as Facebook, and updating your progress publicly.

*Hire Jason as Success and Happiness coach at <u>www.DLUCoaching.com</u>

Challenge #3: Give the Gift of Value

- This book makes an amazing gift. You can make a lasting change in someone's life, especially if that person is in their 20's. At that age, people are trying to figure out life and this could be the catalyst that helps move him or her forward.

- This book would be perfect as a high school or college graduation gift, for a friend who has lost purpose in what they're doing, or for a friend who graduated from college and can't seem to start building their future.

- Who will you share this book with, next?

Challenge #4: Stay Positive

- You will have ups and downs in your journey to grow and improve.

- It's not how many times you fall down that matters; it's how many times you get up. Anytime you are trying something great, you'll have failures.

- Getting ahead in life is not about being perfect.

- Focus on progress, not perfection. You can do this. You have all of the talents and abilities in the world to get to where you want to be. I appreciate you. Even though I may not know you, I believe in you.

Challenge #5: Continue to Grow with www.DailyLifeUniversity.com

- Stay inspired by surrounding yourself with other students of life. No one knows what random social media platform will be popular in 5 or 10 years, but here's where you can currently find *Daily Life University*:

  - Twitter: @DailyLifeU

  - Facebook Group: Daily Life University Community - Students of Life

  - Website: *www.DailyLifeUniversity.com*

  - LinkedIn: Jason Heinritz

  - Instagram: DailyLifeUniversity

  - Snapchat: heinritzjr28

Congratulations again! I can't wait to meet you and get a chance to interact on the facebook group!

ABOUT THE AUTHOR

Since 2004, Jason has delivered over 350 speeches to over 10,000 people, inspiring them to grow professionally and personally. As District Manager at Cutco, he has personally trained over 2,000 representatives and is responsible for over $11 million in sales. In May of 2011, Jason was  recognized as one of the "Future 15" and the first recipient under 30 years old to win this award given to the top 15 young professionals of the Fox Valley area.

He is passionate about sharing his expertise on life-skill development with young people. Through training and mentoring, he helps people develop into better versions of themselves. By teaching personal growth skills including overcoming obstacles, improving communications, time management, goal-setting, and making the right choices, Jason strives to help young people reach their greatest potential.

Jason grew up in Waukesha, WI, where he was very involved in church and sports. He attended college at UW-Whitewater, participating in football and track. In 2008, he graduated with a degree in Sports Management.

In 2004, while still a freshman in college, Jason began his career with Vector Marketing as a representative marketing Cutco Cutlery. He quickly moved up in the company and currently manages the District office in Appleton, WI. Jason is one of the top 500 sales reps of all time in the company's 67-year history. He has risen above the ranks of 1.3 million representatives and has been inducted into the Vector Marketing Hall of Fame.

BOOK JASON AS YOUR NEXT SPEAKER

You can book Jason as your next keynote speaker for students and young professionals. You'll see positive changes as the success secrets and happiness habits that Jason applies on a daily basis are shared in a motivating speech.

Jason Heinritz has been engaging and inspiring audiences for more than 10 years. He has helped thousands with his real and positive messages. Jason can relate to audiences at a level most cannot. He is in the top 1% of performers in his 67-year company history. He has coached thousands of young people to success and has a hunger to continually grow.

Pricing details as of 2018 (prices subject to increase):

- $2,500 for an hour keynote message

- $250 goes to the Front Row Foundation

- $250 goes towards your school's/organization's own *Daily Life University* Scholarship

For more information, please visit: **www.DailyLifeUniversity.com**

GIVE THE GIFT OF VALUE

In 2014 I started giving "gifts of value" as a Christmas gifts. Gifts like personal growth books, subscription to a life-enhancing apps, or free coaching sessions.

This was inexpensive and involved no guesswork, no malls, no long lines, and no hustle and bustle. This book could be more impactful on someone's life than a new video games or iPhone.

If you got anything out of this book, if it shifted your thinking, or inspired you at all, I hope you pass this book along. To improve the world, we need you. Spread the word!

Give this copy or buy a copy for someone else!

WORKS CITED

[1] Jay, Meg. *The Defining Decade: Why Your Twenties Matter — And How to Make the Most of Them Now.* Twelve, 2013.

[2] *Co-Active Wheel of Life.* www.coactive.com/docs/resources/toolkit/pdfs/18-Wheel-of-Life-Exercise.pdf.

[3] *Self Defined Leadership,* selfdefinedleadership.com/blog/.

[4] "Look Up | Gary Turk - Official Video." *YouTube,* 25 Apr. 2014, https://www.youtube.com/watch?v=Z7dLU6fk9QY.

[5] Lecrae. "Sayin Nuthin." *Anomaly,* 2014.

[6] "ISU study finds TV viewing, video game play contribute to kids' attention problems." *RSS,* www.news.iastate.edu/news/2010/jul/TVVGattention.

[7] "Father Guido Sarducci's Five Minute University." *YouTube,* 23 Jan. 2007, https://www.youtube.com/watch?v=kO8x8eoU3L4.

[8] Sparshott, Jeffrey. "Congratulations, Class of 2015. You're the Most Indebted Ever (For Now)." *The Wall Street Journal,* Dow Jones & Company, 8 May 2015, https://blogs.wsj.com/economics/2015/05/08/congratulations-class-of-2015-youre-the-most-indebted-ever-for-now/.

[9] "Trends in College Pricing 2016." *The College Board,* https://trends.collegeboard.org/sites/default/files/2016-trends-college-pricing-web_0.pdf.

[10] Plumer, Brad. "Only 27 percent of college grads have a job related to their major." *The Washington Post,* WP Company, 20 May 2013, https://www.washingtonpost.com/news/wonk/wp/2013/05/20/only-27-percent-of-college-grads-have-a-job-related-to-their-major/?utm_term=.e16410d8a130.

[11] Meister, Jeanne. "The Future Of Work: Job Hopping Is the 'New Normal' for Millennials." *Forbes,* Forbes Magazine, 3 Jan. 2017, https://www.forbes.com/sites/jeannemeister/2012/08/14/the-future-of-work-job-hopping-is-the-new-normal-for-millennials/#5f61160913b8.

[12] Rosensohn, Sam. "Sixty Percent of All College Freshmen Do Not Graduate in Four Years." *College Planning Partnerships ,* https://www.satprepct.com/sixty-percent-of-all-college-freshmen-do-not-graduate-in-four-years/.

[13] "Honest University Commercial." *YouTube*, 21 Feb. 2014, https://www.youtube.com/watch?v=T24DPU-hkJM.

[14] Godin, Seth. *Linchpin: Are you indispensable?* Piatkus, 2011.

[15] Sinek, Simon. *Start with why: how great leaders inspire everyone to take action.* Portfolio/Penguin, 2013.

[16] *NLT Bible.* Proverbs 27:17

[17] Hsieh, Tony. *Delivering happiness: a path to profits, passion, and purpose.* Business Plus, 2013.

[18] Sharma, Robin S. *The monk who sold his Ferrari: a spiritual fable about fulfilling your dreams and reaching your destiny.* Thorsons, 2015.

[19] Ramsey, Dave. *The total money makeover: a proven plan for financial fitness.* Nelson Books, an imprint of Thomas Nelson, 2013.

[20] Kelly, Matthew. *Off balance: getting beyond the work-Life balance myth to personal and professional satisfaction.* Hudson Street Press, 2011.

[21] "Hector and the Pursuit of Happiness." 2014.

[22] Elrod, Hal. *The miracle morning: the not-so-Obvious secret guaranteed to transform your life before 8AM.* Hal Elrod International, Inc., 2016.

[23] Heinritz, Jason. "The Miracle Morning." *Daily Life University*, 1 Oct. 2014, https://dailylifeuniversity.wordpress.com/the-miracle-morning/.

[24] Kendrick, Alex, director. *War Room.* 2015.

[25] "Guided Meditation and Mindfulness - The Headspace App." *Headspace*, https://www.headspace.com/headspace-meditation-app.

[26] "What's your morning ritual?" *Tonyrobbins.com*, 12 Sept. 2017, https://www.headspace.com/headspace-meditation-appwww.tonyrobbins.com/mind-meaning/whats-your-morning-ritual.

[27] Byrne, Rhonda. *The secret: the 10th anniversary edition.* Atria Books, 2016.

[28] Heinritz, Jason. "Daily Affirmations Re-Program your Brain." *Daily Life University*, 11 Aug. 2015, https://dailylifeuniversity.wordpress.com/the-miracle-morning/daily-affirmations-re-program-your-brain/.

29 "Trampolines & Outdoor Play." *Pure Fun*, https://purefun.net/.

30 Maxwell, John C. *The 15 invaluable laws of growth: live them and reach your potential.* Center Street, 2012.

31 Salciccioli, Greg. *The enemies of excellence: 7 reasons why we sabotage success.* Crossroad, 2014.

32 Covey, Stephen R. *The 7 habits of highly effective people: powerful lessons in personal change.* Simon & Schuster, 2014.

33 Sharma, Robin S. *The leader who had no title: an inspiring story about working (and living) at your absolute best.* Simon & Schuster, 2010.

34 Elrod, Hal. *Taking life head on!: the Hal Elrod story: how to love the life you have while you create the life of your dreams.* Hal Elrod International, 2007.

35 Hsieh, Tony. *Delivering happiness: a path to profits, passion, and purpose.* Grand Central Publishing, 2013.

36 Ruiz, Don Miguel. *The Four Agreements: Practical Guide to Personal Freedom.* Amber-Allen Publishing, U.S., 1997.

37 Kelly, Matthew. *The rhythm of life: living every day with passion and purpose.* Beacon, 2015.

38 Hill, Napoleon. *Think and grow rich.* Fawcett Crest, 1960.

40 Kelly, Matthew. *The dream manager.* Hachette Books, 2014.

41 "Five Minute Journal." *Intelligent Change*, www.fiveminutejournal.com/.

42 Cross, Joe and Kurt Engfehr, directors. *Fat, Sick, and Nearly Dead.* 2010.

43 Elrod, Hal. "It Only Takes Five Minutes to Become a Morning Person." *Entrepreneur*, 11 Nov. 2014, https://www.entrepreneur.com/article/238219.

44 Gilkey, Charlie. "When to Swallow Your Daily Frog." *Productive Flourishing*, 3 Apr. 2008, https://www.productiveflourishing.com/when-to-swallow-your-daily-frog/.

45 Stevenson, Shawn. *Sleep smarter: 21 essential strategies to sleep your way to a better body, better health, and bigger success.* Rodale Books, 2016.

46 Shaw, Gina. "Sleep Through the Decades." *WebMD*, WebMD, https://www.webmd.com/sleep-disorders/features/adult-sleep-needs-and-habits.

[47] Maxwell, John C. "John C. Maxwell Facebook Page.", 16 Apr. 2016, https://www.facebook.com/JohnCMaxwell/posts/10154014149332954:0.

[48] "Eric Thomas | ET Inspires." *Eric Thomas | ET Inspires*, http://www.etinspires.com/.

[49] Heinritz, Jason. "Mentality Monday." *Daily Life University*, 14 Nov. 2015, https://dailylifeuniversity.wordpress.com/daily-life-university/thank-god-its-monday/.

[50] "Daily Life University Community - Students of Life." *Daily Life University Community - Students of Life Public Group*, https://www.facebook.com/groups/635380616536102/.

[51] Fulkerson, Lee, director. *Forks Over Knives*. 2011.

[52] Kenner, Robert, director. *Food, Inc.* 2008.

[53] Spurlock, Morgan, director. *Supersize Me.* 2004.

[54] Colquhoun, James, et al., directors. *Hungry For Change*. 2012.

[55] "Food, Inc." *TakePart*, 22 Jan. 2015, www.takepart.com/foodinc/.

[56] *Prevent Disease.Com - Aiming Towards Better Health*. preventdisease.com/.

[57] Cuilty, James, and Maya Gottfried. "Forks Over Knives." *Forks Over Knives*, www.forksoverknives.com/.

[58] *Panna*, www.pannacooking.com/.

[59] "The Cutco Kitchen." *The Cutco Kitchen*, www.cutcokitchen.com/.

[60] *Mind Body Green*, www.mindbodygreen.com/.

[61] Heinritz, Jason. "The Dirty 30 – Is your life a HALF, a THIRD, or just a FOURTH over when you turn 30?" *Daily Life University*, 23 Nov. 2014, https://dailylifeuniversity.wordpress.com/2014/11/07/the-dirty-30-is-your-life-a-half-a-third-or-just-a-fourth-over-when-you-turn-30/.

[62] Heinritz, Jason. "Wellness Wednesday." *Daily Life University*, 27 Sept. 2015, http://dailylifeuniversity.wordpress.com/daily-life-university/wellness-wednesday/.

[63] Elrod, Hal. "Ep. #23: Three Keys to Emotional Intelligence." *HalElrod.com*, 14 Aug. 2014, https://halelrod.com/ep-23-three-keys-to-emotional-intelligence/.

[64] Ni, Preston. "How to Increase Your Emotional Intelligence — 6 Essentials." *Psychology Today*, Sussex Publishers, 5 Oct. 2014, www.psychologytoday.com/blog/communication-

success/201410/how-increase-your-emotional-intelligence-6-essentials.

[65] Chapman, Gary D. *The Five Love Languages*. Manjul Pub., 2010.

[66] Ramsey, Dave. "Financial Peace University." *Financial Peace University /DaveRamsey.Com*, www.daveramsey.com/fpu.

[67] Cruze, Rachel. *Rachel Cruze*, www.rachelcruze.com/.

[68] Heinritz, Jason. "How to Cover Your Expenses and Stay Out of Debt in College." *Daily Life University*, 9 Oct. 2015, https://dailylifeuniversity.wordpress.com/2015/10/07/how-to-cover-your-expenses-and-stay-out-of-debt-in-college/.

[69] *Mint: Money Manager, Bills, Credit Score & Budgeting*. www.Mint.com.

[70] Kelly, Matthew. *The rhythm of life: living every day with passion and purpose*. Beacon, 2015.

[71] Voogd, Peter J. *Peter J Voogd*, https://peterjvoogd.com/about/.

[72] *YouVersion*, www.youversion.com/.

[73] Filkouski, Alex. *Google Calendar*.

[74] *Marc Levy Quotes*. www.goodreads.com/author/quotes/61788.Marc_Levy.

[75] Kelly, Matthew. *Become the Best Version of Yourself by Matthew Kelly*. YouTube, 16 Mar. 2016, www.youtube.com/watch?v=v44jxQDYb9M.

[76] *KJV Bible*. Proverbs 29:18

[77] Batterson, Mark. *Circle maker*. Zondervan, 2016.

[78] *Quotes by J.C. Penny*. www.goodreads.com/quotes/574812-give-me-a-stock-clerk-with-a-goal-and-i.

[79] Elrod, Hal. "Ep. #3: How to Implement and Sustain Any Habit." *HalElrod.com*, 18 May 2014, halelrod.com/040/.

SELF-PUBLISHING
SCHOOL

NOW IT'S YOUR TURN

Discover the EXACT 3-step blueprint you need to become a bestselling author in 3 months.

Self-Publishing School helped me, and now I want them to help you with this FREE VIDEO SERIES!

Even if you're busy, bad at writing, or don't know where to start, you CAN write a bestseller and build your best life.

With tools and experience across a variety niches and professions, Self-Publishing School is the <u>only</u> resource you need to take your book to the finish line!

DON'T WAIT

Watch this FREE VIDEO SERIES now, and
Say "YES" to becoming a bestseller:

https://xe172.isrefer.com/go/curcust/heinritzjr28

Made in the USA
Middletown, DE
25 April 2018